Public Relati

This unique
gives the rea
of organizati
relations prac
both in public

This secor
edition to offe
and the devel

- The use of
- the growin
- local autho
- high profil
- sports spo
- property s

Featuring cas
Croatia and t
students worl

Danny Mos
Chester, UK.

Melanie Pow
University, UK

Public Relations Cases

International perspectives

**Edited by Danny Moss
and Melanie Powell
with Barbara DeSanto**

Routledge
Taylor & Francis Group

LONDON AND NEW YORK

First published 2010
by Routledge
2 Park Square, Milton Park, Abingdon, Oxon OX14 4RN

Simultaneously published in the USA and Canada
by Routledge
270 Madison Ave, New York, NY 10016

Routledge is an imprint of the Taylor & Francis Group, an Informa business

© 2010 Danny Moss and Melanie Powell

Typeset in Amasis by
Swales & Willis Ltd, Exeter, Devon
Printed and bound in Great Britain by
TJ International Ltd, Padstow, Cornwall

British Library Cataloguing in Publication Data
A catalogue record for this book is available from the British Library

Library of Congress Cataloging-in-Publication Data
Public relations cases : international perspectives/edited by Danny Moss,
Melanie Powell & Barbara DeSanto. – 2nd ed.
        p. cm.
    Includes bibliographical references and index.
    1. Public relations–Case studies.   2. Public relations–Cross-cultural
studies.   3. Corporations–Public relations–Case studies.   4. International
business enterprises–Case studies.   I. Moss, Danny, 1954–   II. Powell,
Melanie.   III. DeSanto, Barbara, 1950–
HM1221.P78 2010
659.2–dc22   2009036140

ISBN: 978–0–415–77336–2 (hbk)
ISBN: 978–0–415–77337–9 (pbk)
ISBN: 978–0–203–08898–2 (ebk)

For Angus, my much-loved golden retriever,
who sadly left us before this book could be finished,
but whose spirit and smiling face are constantly with me.

Contents

Figures

Notes on contributors

LISA ASHURST

Lisa Ashurst, MA is a public relations consultant and was head of communications for property developer Urban Splash for six years until November 2008. In the years she worked there, the company rose from a niche northern outfit to the leading regeneration company in the UK.

As head of communications Lisa was responsible for all of the organization's PR, including media relations, exhibitions and events and public consultations. She also wrote the monthly email newsletter, handled corporate communications and developed PR strategies, working in partnership with many public sector organizations.

Before joining Urban Splash, Lisa worked for Laing Construction (now known as Laing O'Rourke), working on some of the most high profile building projects in Manchester, including the City of Manchester Stadium for the 2002 Commonwealth Games, the extension of Manchester's Metrolink tram line, the remodelling of Manchester Piccadilly train station and the rebuilding of the Arndale Food Court, which was damaged by the IRA bomb in 1996.

Originally from Astley near Wigan, Lisa lives in Manchester city centre. She has a Master's Degree in Public Relations from Manchester Metropolitan University. She is also chair of New Islington Festival, a free family festival held annually in Manchester, and a mentor to students on the PR course. In her spare time Lisa can usually be found watching bands and generally enjoying herself.

RYAN BOWD

Ryan Bowd is Head of SBI Active, at IMG Consulting, a sponsorship and PR consultancy that is part of the IMG group. IMG Consulting clients include Asics, Abu Dhabi Tourist Authority, British Airways, Cadbury, Gatorade, GE, and the Times newspaper.

Ryan is an award winning PR practitioner who mixes a professional life of communications practice with academic teaching and learning. Ryan is currently undertaking PhD research on the subject of corporate social responsibility communications. Prior to his current post, Ryan worked for Leeds Metropolitan University, Manchester Metropolitan University, Leeds University, Weber Shandwick Public Relations, Connectpoint PR and 1090 Communications. His current and past clients include AstraZeneca, Shell, Adidas Eyewear, Countryside Properties, Gatorade (PepsiCo brand), The Salford Triathlon World Cup Triathlon, Major Public Relations Consultancies, The National Lottery in the Northwest and other corporate, consumer, luxury/design and sporting clients. Research interests include the fields of reputation, corporate social responsibility (CSR) and communications.

ROB BROWN

Rob graduated in Economics and Politics and spent a year in radio before going into PR. He set up his own company in the 1990s, working with ITV, Channel Four and Endemol. He sold the company to Leedex. In 1999 he left Leedex to join McCann Erickson as PR Director. In 2008 he joined Staniforth as UK Managing Director. Clients include Marks and Spencer, Nissan and Kellogg's. He is the author of *Public Relations and the Social Web* (2009).

RONNIE BROWN

Ronnie Brown has worked in marketing for 12 years, eight of them being specifically within digital marketing. Currently the Marketing and Account Director at Outside Line, Ronnie has previously held roles at EMI Music and Reed Exhibitions. He is fascinated by the accurate measurement of social media and the demise of his beloved Southampton FC; he can talk at length about both. Ronnie lives in south west London with his wife Jaime and daughter Beau.

GERALD CHAN

Gerald Chan is Head of Communications and External Affairs at the Royal College of Obstetricians and Gynaecologists (RCOG). He oversees the RCOG's media and public relations office and manages its communications with Parliament. Previously, he was Head of Education Policy at the Chartered Institute of Public Relations in London.

BILL DARING

Bill Daring, who died in 2009, was Chairman and CEO of KMP, one of the most successful independent digital agencies in the UK. Bill was responsible for developing new business and KMP's strategic and technical partnerships.

He founded KMP in 1991, after over a decade in the advertising and PR industry. During the late 1990s, KMP pioneered the use of multimedia in websites. Macromedia commissioned KMP to build the Shockwave website, which was the precursor of Flash. In 1997 he established one of the most successful biotechnology community sites, biofind.com. It was a web 2.0 pioneer and is still the market leader today.

Bill's most recent interests were social media, web 2.0 applications and PR 2.0. KMP recently launched PressRoom, a social media release template which quickly became a basic PR 2.0 tool for PR agencies.

TOM EARL

Tom Earl is Head of PR and New Business for SBI – a sponsorship and PR consultancy that is part of the IMG group. Their main clients include HSBC, John Smith's, Robinsons, Citroen and the *Times* newspaper.

Before that, he was Sponsorship Manager for attheraces, the horse racing rights holder, broadcaster and betting company, between 2002 and 2004.

He began his career in the sponsorship industry with SBI (again) in the spring of 2000, when his clients included Cisco Systems and the *Daily Telegraph*.

Following a 2:1 in French and Italian at Exeter University, Tom spent three years as a ski and summer sports instructor and resort manager in Switzerland, Italy and France.

ROBBIE HUSTON

Robbie Huston manages government relations for Sellafield Ltd. He has several years of experience managing communications issues and stakeholder relations, including international relations and parliamentary affairs.

From 2000–2005 he was a participant in the BNFL Stakeholder Dialogue, facilitated by the Environment Council. Previously, having served an engineering apprenticeship, he spent 18 years as a shop steward and site convenor at BNFL's Capenhurst uranium enrichment plant. As a mature student, he gained first class honours in Political Science at Liverpool John Moores University in 1997.

JEEYOON LEE

Jeeyoon Lee has been working as a Senior Vice President at Fleishman-Hillard Korea. She has extensive experience in global campaigns and issues management for multinational companies and various public awareness campaigns for the Korean government. Much of her work focuses on communications strategy, stakeholder management and issues management. She received her BA in French Language and Literature from Sogang University in Seoul, Korea and received the Public Relations Certificate from Emerson College in Boston, US.

HYUNKI MOON

Hyunki Moon has been in the advertising industry for 16 years and the PR industry for three years. His career experience of working in both advertising and PR agencies and working in both account service and creative in advertising is quite unique in nature and can rarely be found in the communication industry in Korea. Currently, he is a doctoral student majoring public relations at Hankuk University of Foreign Studies in Seoul, Korea.

DANNY MOSS

Dr Danny Moss has recently become Professor of Corporate and Public Affairs at the University of Chester. Previously he was Director of the Centre for Corporate and Public Affairs at the Manchester Metropolitan University Business School, and Programme Leader for the University's Master's Degree in International Public Relations. Before moving to MMUBS, he was Director of Public Relations programmes at the University of Stirling, where he established the first dedicated Master's Degree in Public Relations in the UK. He is also the co-organizer of Bledcom, the annual Global Public Relations Research Symposium which is held in Lake Bled, Slovenia. Dr Moss is the author of a number of journal articles and books, including *Public Relations Research: An International Perspective* (co-edited with Toby MacManus and Dejan Vercic), *Perspectives on Public Relations Research* (co-edited with Dejan Vercic and Gary Warnaby) and *Public Relations Cases: International Perspectives* (co-edited with Barbara DeSanto).

PETER OSBORNE

Peter Osborne, MCIPR, MA (PR), BA (Hons) has more than 20 years of PR experience in the nuclear (BNFL) and water industries (United Utilities), where he is currently a public affairs manager. He has operational and site experience of managing corporate press offices and internal communications. His international public relations experience includes public information missions to Australia, New Zealand and Fiji, where he liaised with government and media over nuclear transports. He was European Media Affairs Manager for BNFL's European nuclear transports.

A former journalist and accredited CIPR practitioner, he is a visiting speaker to the MSc in International Public Relations at MMUBS, where he took his MA in PR.

MELANIE POWELL

Melanie Powell, MA, MPhil, MCIPR is a senior lecturer at Manchester Metropolitan University Business School, where she is Programme Tutor for the MSc International Public Relations and Programme Leader for the CIPR Diploma, as well as a leader of units in marketing communications theory and creative brand strategy at undergraduate level. Previously, she was a senior lecturer in Public Relations at Leeds Metropolitan University Business School. Before becoming an academic in 1996, she spent 14 years as a practitioner in local authority public relations and in arts marketing.

YUNNA RHEE

Dr Yunna Rhee is an associate professor in the Division of Communication, Hankuk University of Foreign Studies, Seoul, Korea, where she teaches theories in public relations, international public relations and strategic public relations planning. Prior to joining Hankuk University, she was an assistant professor at California State University, Sacramento. She received her PhD from the University of Maryland, College Park. She has published articles and book chapters on employee communication, global public relations, and strategic relationship management.

GANGA S. DHANESH

Ganga Sasidharan Dhanesh is a doctoral student in communication management at the Communications and New Media Programme at the National University of Singapore. She holds a Master's Degree in Business Administration from the Cochin University of Science and Technology, India and has had experience in human resources management and corporate communication in corporate and non-profit organizations. She has co-authored a book for non-native speakers of English, *Speak English in Four Easy Steps*. She started her doctoral studies in January 2007. Her current research explores the intersection of public relations and corporate social responsibility.

RONNIE SEMLEY

Ronnie Semley, Dip CIPR, MCIR, is Communications and Media Manager in Bolton Council's Communications and Marketing Agency. As part of the Agency's manage-ment team and in working with Sue Strange, the council's Assistant Director of Communications and Marketing, he helped to coordinate the introduction and subsequent development of the award-winning Bolton place brand, launched in 2005. The Bolton brand case is based on an unpublished research project written by Ronnie for the CIPR Diploma in 2007.

GEOFF SIMPSON

Geoff Simpson, FCIPR is an independent public relations consultant. He began his career as a business journalist and later spent 15 years as Public Affairs Manager at what is now The Co-operative Group. Over many years Geoff has researched the

Battle of Britain, including talking to and corresponding with several hundred of the RAF aircrew who took part. He is a trustee of the Battle of Britain Memorial Trust.

MAJDA TAFRA-VLAHOVIĆ

Dr Majda Tafra-Vlahović, MCIPR, divides her time between teaching at the University of Dubrovnik and Zagreb BAK Management College and consulting. She is an associate of the Sustainability Advisory Group. She has spent most of her career in senior management positions in UNICEF and Coca-Cola, dealing with human rights, corporate social responsibility, public affairs and communication. She holds a PhD in information sciences, two postgraduate certificates in sustainable business from the University of Cambridge and the Diploma and an Accredited Practitioner certificate from the UK Chartered Institute of Public Relations (CIPR). She lives in Zagreb, Croatia.

SIMON TORP

Dr Simon Torp is Vice-Head and Associate Professor in Strategic Communication at the Department of Marketing and Management at the University of Southern Denmark. He has a PhD in Business Administration and a Master's Degree in Philosophy and Organizational Culture and Communication. His current responsibilities include being Director of the programme in Marketing, Branding and Communication and PhD coordinator for the department. He has acted as a consultant in the sphere of communication, management and intercultural understanding in Danish and international companies.

Introduction

DANNY MOSS, MELANIE POWELL AND BARBARA DESANTO

It might seem that the world of public relations (PR) is changing at an ever more rapid rate, particularly in recent years, yet at the same time the fundamental purpose and role of public relations arguably has changed very little. Indeed, the more we look at the practice around the world, many common elements can be observed as well as some notable differences, whether it be in the Far East, United States, Europe or South America. Such commonality and variation in understanding and practice are perhaps only to be expected given that public relations has evolved from different starting points, and in some cases under vastly different environmental conditions. Indeed, Sriramesh and Vercic (2003) point to the steadily evolving nature of the public relations industry around the world, highlighting the profession's coming of age in many parts the world as a result of increasing democratization and economic liberalization. One can also point to the influence of the large global consultancies and multinational corporations that have directly or indirectly helped spread ideas and knowledge of public relations practice throughout the developed and developing world.

Here researchers have sought to identify those contextual factors that may account for differences in the way public relations is understood and practised in different countries. The political system and political climate in a country or region, media ownership and media structures, social values and norms and economic conditions are all factors that have been shown to influence the way in which public relations has developed and is practised (see Sriramesh and Vercic 2003). Moreover, within individual countries, there may often be significant regional differences in dialects, cultural norms and mores. All of these may have quite profound implications for the role and work of public relations practitioners. Arguably, the increasing internationalization of business has brought with it a concomitant growth of interest and focus on internationalizing public relations practice. This changing emphasis can be seen not only in the communications or public relations functions of the larger multinational companies, but also within the larger and smaller consultancies, where cultural sensitivity has become an increasing necessity in developing successful strategies for clients of all sizes.

PURPOSE VERSUS TECHNIQUES

While there may be broad acceptance of the proposition that the way public relations is understood and practised may vary in different parts of the world, acceptance of such a proposition may arguably obscure an important distinction between the purpose or the ends to which public relations may be directed, and the means or techniques employed to achieve those ends. Research into international public relations has shown quite marked variations in the understanding of the purpose or the ends to which public relations may be directed in different national, regional or local settings. However, what such research also often reveals is that the actual techniques or activities that practitioners may utilize in pursuit of these ends may not vary that greatly around the world.

THE IMPACT OF THE WEB AND SOCIAL MEDIA

While the array of communication techniques may manifest themselves in slightly different ways around the world (i.e. the form and protocols associated with media relations work), almost irrespective of where practitioners are based, a broadly similar set of communications techniques can be found in use (e.g. events, media relations, various types of publications, video/DVD and, increasingly, web-based communication). Perhaps the one driver that has begun to transform the day-to-day practice of public relations is the increasingly pervasive presence of the Internet and social media in particular. The global reach of the Internet and of social media has transformed the way in which many individuals gather information, seek out news, form opinions and even contribute to news generation themselves (through a variety of websites and mechanisms such as blogging and the posting of messages and images on social media sites such as Facebook and YouTube). Significantly, these new online media channels have become increasing powerful tools in mobilizing support for particular causes or, as was seen in the most recent US Presidential election, in political campaigning. Of course, their influence has transformed the way an increasing number of people purchase goods and services. Indeed, the rapid growth of the Internet and social media around the world has transformed, on one hand, the dynamic between the news creators and disseminators, and, on the other hand, the news consumers. Recognizing this changing dynamic, many public relations firms and in-house departments have already begun to integrate Internet and social media-based elements into their communications strategies. Moreover, these changes are not confined to just the Western world. These changes are becoming an increasingly important factor in developing communications virtually everywhere in the world.

SOCIAL RESPONSIBILITY

Another increasingly internationally observable trend in recent years has been the surge of interest in corporate responsibility and corporate governance. Even before the advent of the recent so-called 'credit crunch' and worldwide recession, societal expectations of big business had begun to change significantly. The high profile collapse of the European banking group Barings and the demise of Enron in the USA, both of which were attributed to malpractice and corruption, heralded a call for greater regulation and more stringent governance in the corporate sector. These high-profile corporate failures exposed further concerns about the behaviour and polices of some of the world's largest businesses. These concerns have been coupled with wider global concerns over the impact of business and mankind as a whole on the planet's ecosystem and, in particular, on climate change. Against this backdrop, there has been an upsurge of interest in the concept of corporate social responsibility as a manifestation of businesses' recognition of the need to respond to the growing pressures being exerted on them by governments and a range of pressure groups demanding that businesses act in a more accountable and responsible manner.

These two trends in particular – the growth of the Internet and social media and the increased importance attached to corporate social responsibility – are reflected in a number of cases contained in this book. Other cases in this book provide valuable insights into the broad complexion of contemporary public relations practice, providing both students and practitioners of public relations with useful lessons about how public relations can used effectively in a variety of contexts.

THE CASES

The cases written by Ronnie Brown (Case 4) and also Bill Daring (Case 1) offer valuable insights into the ways in which organizations can exploit the rapid growth of interest in social media and the Internet. The cases demonstrate the versatility and potentially powerful reach and influence of these new social media channels.

In Case 8, Rob Brown explores the challenges of transforming a public relations agency to respond to the changing online media landscape and growing demand for digital communications in particular.

Yunna Rhee, Hyunki Moon and Jeeyoon Lee (Case 5), Peter Osborne amd Robbie Huston (Case 6) and Majda Tafra-Vlahović (Case 12) offer valuable insights into how major international companies have attempted to build dialogue and understanding with their stakeholders at national and local levels, thereby reinforcing their posi-tioning as responsible corporate citizens. These cases examine the challenges and approaches to corporate stakeholder relationship-building activity in three very different con-texts: Korea, the UK and Croatia. They illustrate how cultural and other contextual differences may affect the way organizations go about the building stakeholder relationships.

Ryan Bowd (Case 2) and Tom Earl (Case 9) demonstrate the varied application and potential of sports sponsorship. This is demonstarted in the former case as part of an international profile and funding raising campaign on behalf of Cancer Research and in the latter case by strengthening the brand profile and customer franchise for a major brewer. In Case 11, Simon Torp reexamines the long-standing tension between public relations and marketing functions. He reviews how an understanding, or a lack of understanding, of the two functions can prove highly problematic when an organization attempts structural integration of the two functions.

Gerald Chan (Case 7), rather than examining a particular campaign, offers a fascinating insight into the challenges of developing and maintaining a public relations function within a long-established and very traditional professional medical body.

Geoff Simpson (Case 10) examines the role of public relations around a major commemorative event: the RAF 's role during the Battle of Britain in the Second World War.

Ganga Dhanesh (Case 3) examines the major impact of an award winning tourism promotional campaign on behalf of Kerala, a small state in the south western corner of India. Dhanesh illustrates just how powerful a tool public relations can be when applied effectively.

Ronnie Semley and Melanie Powell (Case 12) also focus on the public sector, but in this case they explore one of the most memorable and successful brand building campaigns for a local authority in the UK.

Finally, in Case 14, Lisa Ashurst explores how public relations was used to attract and build overwhelming interest in an innovative new housing scheme that had been developed in a previously deprived and problematic part of Salford in Greater Manchester.

We believe that collectively these cases provide a varied and valuable set of insights into how contemporary public relations can be used successfully to support organizational goals across a range of different organizational and cultural contexts.

TRIBUTE: BILL DARING

Finally, it is with great sadness that all three editors announce that Bill Daring died suddenly at the end of 2009, before this collection was published. Bill's case is a testament to his creativity and ability to engage his audience. We are proud to acknowledge this by placing Bill's case as the first in the book.

1

Take a look at my giraffe

Promoting Chester Zoo

BILL DARING

Chester Zoo is home to 7,000 animals and 400 different species. It is the UK's number one zoo. As a long-established national favourite, by 2007 Chester Zoo found itself operating in an increasingly competitive world and it was forced it to embrace the new web technologies and digital PR.

Figure 1.1 Giraffe

BACKGROUND

KMP were contracted to build Chester Zoo's new website in 2007. We developed a new design and implemented the Sitecore content management system. It enabled several editor groups within Chester Zoo, such as marketing, education, conservationists and keepers, to update the site content (i.e. pictures and text) easily.

In addition to the animal pages, news and visitor attractions, the challenge was to engage Chester Zoo's web audience (i.e. friends and visitors) in an interactive relationship from which a dialogue and strengthening loyalty with Chester Zoo could be built. At this time photo-sharing was seen as being on the fringes of social media and we were uncertain as to how it could be used in a digital PR campaign. The sole objective of the web campaign in the beginning was to encourage a greater number of web users to visit Chester Zoo. In the previous year there had been approximately one million visitors to Chester Zoo, but less than 3,000 unique visitors per month to the website.

WHAT IS SOCIAL MEDIA?

The concept of social media probably started to evolve in 2004 when blogging started to become popular and social networking sites such as Facebook and MySpace were launched on the digital arena. Consumers had become more active in their internet usage; no longer content to surf the net, they wanted to become more involved through conversations and contributions. Youngsters were abandoning traditional

Figure 1.2 Chester Zoo website

media in favour of new media, spending time on MSN, in chat rooms, and on social networking sites such as Facebook, MySpace, Bebo, forums and blogs.

Commercial sites such as eBay, Amazon, Trip Advisor and Moneysavingexpert.com had started to champion user contributions and bulletin boards. Consumers wanted to exchange views with like-minded internet users. Social media was born and was starting to take off.

Now nearly half of the online adult population around the world is a member of at least one networking site. Facebook and MySpace jointly house more than 170 million monthly active users. The goal for the business world was how to tap into this potential customer base. Businesses now have access to 500 million active internet users through the media. Photo-sharing sites such as Flickr and Photobucket have become major players in the social networking space. They are perpetuated by consumers' desire to share photographs and engage in conversations about the photos.

COMMUNICATION STRATEGY

Photo-sharing is the publishing or transfering of a user's digital photos online, thus enabling the user to publicly or privately share them with others. This functionality is

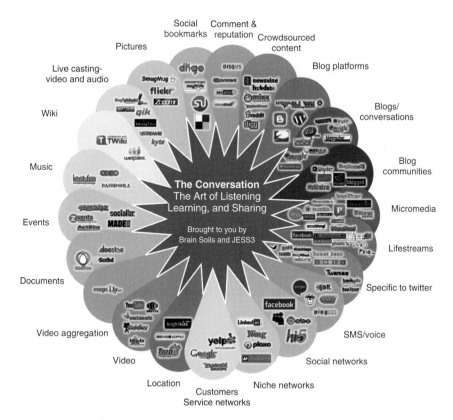

Figure 1.3 Range of internet options

provided through websites and applications that facilitate the uploading and displaying of images. The term can also be loosely applied to the use of online photo galleries that are set up and managed by individual users, including photoblogs.

The first photo-sharing sites originated during the mid to late 1990s primarily from sites providing online ordering of prints (i.e. photo finishing). Many more came into being during the early 2000s with the goal of providing permanent and centralized access to a user's photos and, in some cases, video clips too. Flickr was one of the first, having been created in 2002 by Caterina Fake and Stewart Butterfield. This has resulted in different approaches to revenue generation and functionality among providers.

While photoblogs tend only to display a chronological view of user-selected medium-sized photos, most photo-sharing sites provide multiple views (such as thumbnails and slideshows), the ability to classify photos into albums and the ability to add annotations (e.g. captions or tags) and comments. Some photo sharing sites provide complete online organization tools which are equivalent to desktop photo-management applications.

During our research into what visitors do when they visit Chester Zoo, we realized that photography or, more specifically, photo-sharing could be used to Chester Zoo's advantage. We believed that if we educated and encouraged people to upload pictures to the Chester Zoo site and hold those pictures on a stable photo-sharing

Figure 1.4 Photo sharing on Chester Zoo website

network site such as Flickr, it would foster interactive conversations and discovery about the Chester Zoo brand. Moreover, when we started to investigate the Flickr site as a potential medium for photo-sharing, we discovered that the word 'zoo' was in the top 50 key search terms.

Back in 2007 we took a chance that the phenomenon of photo-sharing would take off. Industry data later released in November 2008 proved that our gamble had paid off. The data showed that of the 500 million daily active internet users, 62 per cent announced that they were engaged in photo-sharing.

As part of the initial website build we designed and built a photo upload section to encourage user contributions and interaction. By uploading their own photos to the website users would agree to allow Chester Zoo to publish the photograph on line and in any subsequent zoo publicity. Once moderated by the content editors, the photo would be automatically marked with a chesterzoo.org watermark in the bottom right-hand corner before being posted to the Chester Zoo community area on the Flickr website.

The return on investment would be delivered simply by the acquisition of thousands of great animal photos taken by the public for Chester Zoo to use in its publicity. However, in a wider context, the chesterzoo.org watermark being placed on all the uploaded photos posted to the Flickr group allowed the brand to have a wide reach and to be distributed globally through the download of the photographs from the internet via the search engines and the Flickr.com site. This in turn would lead to links back to the Chester Zoo website.

A social media platform should build communication and exist for the benefit of the people in the community. As initiator of communication, a business can only influence communication if they are prepared to accept and are favourable towards that business input. We knew we had to be careful of how to engage in communication

Salvador moniter lizard

Visit Chester Zoo

Uploaded on May 14, 2009
0 comments

Figure 1.5 Salvador monitor lizard

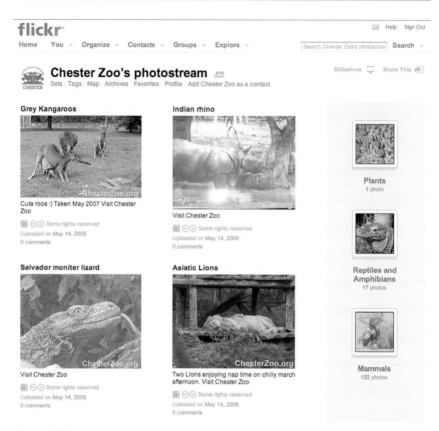

Figure 1.6 Photostream

as we wished to avoid alienating any member of that community. We were also acutely aware that communities can be lost as quickly as they can be built. We were aiming at an existing visitor audience and needed to engage them through photo-sharing. The first step was to ensure that the consumer was engaged, interest on a commercial level would come later. After launching the photo-sharing campaign, Chester Zoo received thousands of photographs. Beyond our expectations, many of the photographs were excellent and were of a professional standard.

By agreeing to our conditions of upload, these photographs could be used for Chester Zoo's publicity. With 400 different species in Chester Zoo, commissioning photographs of them was not only extremely costly but a logistical nightmare. Here we had a talented and interested target audience who were willing and proud to share their creativity.

As the campaign developed, we realized that Chester Zoo was building a platform for top amateurs and professional photographers to showcase their work. Chester Zoo's website's terms and conditions gave copyright to Chester Zoo. The photographer's work was exposed to an international audience through the web.

TARGET AUDIENCE

Originally, we thought our target audience would be any visitors who took photo-graphs while visiting Chester Zoo. As the campaign gathered momentum, we realized that the audience extended from enthusiastic amateurs to professional photographers who were building, strengthening or extending their portfolios. Animal photography is a specialist interest and many serious and professional photographers consider it a vital element in a photographic portfolio.

Our target audience can be split into two main categories:

* voyeurs and
* contributors.

Voyeurs were defined as people searching for specific animal photos on the Flickr website or simply just friends of Chester Zoo looking at animal photography. Contributors were defined as Chester Zoo photography contributors (i.e. amateurs, semi-professionals or professionals) who contributed either via the photo upload functionality on the Chester Zoo website or directly to their own accounts or un-official groups on Flickr.com. Interestingly, voyeurs could become contributors once they developed confidence and skills. Alternatively, a contributor could also be a voyeur, watching and commenting on what others were uploading on to the Chester Zoo site.

THE CAMPAIGN

The campaign started as soon as we launched the website. By placing a Flickr widget on the home page, we encouraged our target audience to upload photographs to the Chester Zoo website. We kept an eye on the 'Chester Zoo' tags listed on Flickr.com. As the official Chester Zoo group on Flickr started to grow (fed by the website uploads), we noticed that other items tagged with 'Chester Zoo' but posted on individual accounts held on Flickr also grew. Commentary began to develop on some of these collections. We soon realized that the content editors not only needed to upload photographic content to the Flickr site, but they also needed to engage with the blogs to stimulate dialogue about the uploaded photographs.

What were the stories behind the photographs? Was the subject an endangered species? Was there something special about the composition or lighting of the photograph?

It was soon evident that with the volume of photographs posted, moderation was becoming a huge task and added resources needed to be enlisted to cope.

Through this online media, the campaign aimed to increase awareness and interest in the Chester Zoo brand and its website, as well as encourage new visitors to Chester Zoo and provide a catalogue of quality photographs which could be used in publicity.

Figure 1.7 Orangutan portal

RESULTS AND EVALUATION

In just one year, over 2,000 photographs were uploaded via the Chester Zoo website. On Flickr there were 32,000 items tagged with 'Chester Zoo'. Most of these items have stimulated at least one conversation, but they typically attract between ten and 200 comments, proving that social engagement has taken place.

With regard to the benefits to Search Engine Marketing (SEM), the site visitor statistics show that the traffic to the site has more than doubled. In 2009, unique visitors peaked at 10,000 per day during holiday periods and regularly exceeded 4,000 visits per day. Flickr.com ranks around 40 in the referral sites, delivering approximately 50 leads to the site per month. Ticket sales and gate sales have increased with total visitor sales rising by almost 30 per cent in the period.

Chester Zoo has also been able to use these photographs in its marketing publicity. The use of the photographs has achieved:

- a major saving in professional photography fees
- and continued engagement of the target audience.

Further evidence can be seen by searching for 'Chester Zoo' in Google Images. The Chester Zoo watermark being displayed on photographs achieves the objective

Photo Gallery

If you have digital photos from Chester Zoo that you would like to share with us, please send them to us using the upload page.

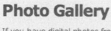 your Photos   Photo Search [   ] GO»

Figure 1.8
Otters

Red Pandas

Young Red Pandas at play

Visit Chester Zoo

Comments

 somesai are says:
Please consider adding this photo to PandasUnlimited.
Posted 13 months ago. (permalink)

 christine_lucas2008 says:
Aww wish I could have seen them playing when I went in May
Posted 6 months ago. (permalink)

Would you like to comment?

Sign up for a free account, or sign in (if you're already a member).

Figure 1.9 Red Pandas

Figure 1.10 Chester Zoo on Google

of widely distributing Chester Zoo's logo to both a national and international audience.

The challenge for Chester Zoo now is to engage its on-line photography audiences as a separate group. For example, special photographers' days have been proposed to bring the community physically together so that they can develop their relationships with each other and with Chester Zoo. It is envisaged that Chester Zoo will hold special events which will be geared to the Flickr audiences, such as particular animal exhibits, photography talks, photography exhibitions, photographic competitions, etc.

Another suggestion is that on a larger scale Chester Zoo could organize safari photographic holidays to visit the zoo's conservation centres around the world to further encourage interest and strengthen the community's relationship.

As social media continues to mature, we constantly evaluate social groups and their engagement with Chester Zoo. The role of other social media, such as Twitter, Facebook, MySpace, Bebo, YouTube and blogs is under investigation as platforms for engagement within the zoo community. In the same way as we have developed the photo-sharing facility, we propose building a similar platform for video uploads. We suggest the host for these shared videos should be either YouTube or a Vimeo channel.

LESSONS LEARNED

The Chester Zoo photo-sharing campaign has attracted thousands of participants. There is a burgeoning community out there that needs to be managed and developed to commercial advantage. Any social media campaign, including photo-sharing, is a two-way process and the organization must understand its responsibilities.

In order to sustain an effective campaign, an organization must:

- maintain the engagement and enthusiasm of the contributing photographers who want to see their work displayed on Flickr's Chester Zoo group;
- have the necessary resources in place to manage the output of the community;
- adapt to changes with imagination.

Social media is the new arm of PR and conversations need to be monitored as an indicator of brand effectiveness. Once that achievement has been measured, the organization can look to digital innovation to satisfy their increasingly sophisticated followers.

ADDITIONAL READING

Brown, F. (2007) 'Metadata Goes Mainstream — about online photo galleries and the lessons we can learn', *KnowGenesis International Journal for Technical Communication*, Volume 2 Issue 1 March.

Gilbertson, S. (2007) 'Give Your Photos Coffee Table Glory With Flickr And Blurb', *Chicago Tribune*, 19 June. Available at: http://blog.wired.com/monkeybites/2007/06/give_your_ photo.html [Accessed 1 June 2009].

Speroni di Fenizio, P. (2005) 'On Tag Clouds, Metric, Tag Sets and Power Laws', P.S. Post Scriptum weblog posting, 25 May. Available at: http://blog.pietrosperoni.it/2005/05/25/ tag-clouds-metric/ [Accessed 1 June 2009].

Stevens, H. (2008) 'Websites offer bits of wisdom', *Chicago Tribune*, 18 August. Available at: http://newsok.com/article/3284234/print=1 [Accessed 1 July 2009].

Wednet (2009) 'Disposable Wedding Cameras'. Available at: http://www.wednet.com/ wedding-photography/wedding-articles/Disposable-Wedding-Cameras.Aspx [Accessed 1 June 2009].

Vanderwal, T. (2005) 'Explaining and Showing Broad and Narrow Folksonomies', *Personal Infocloud* weblog posting, 21 February. Available at: http://personalinfocloud.com/2005/ 02/explaining_and_.html [Accessed 1 June 2009].

WEB REFERENCES

http://www.chesterzoo.org
http://www.chesterzoo.org/Photos.aspx
http://www.flickr.com/photos/8488209@N07

http://www.flickr.com/search/?q=chester+zoo
http://www.kmp.co.uk
http://www.scribd.com
http://www.vnu.net
http://www.twitter.com
http://www.youtube.com

2

Jane's Ride Across America

RYAN BOWD AND MELANIE POWELL

BACKGROUND

Jane Tomlinson MBE (2003) from Rothwell, Leeds, England was diagnosed with breast cancer when she was 26 years old. After being told she was suffering from incurable cancer, Jane inspired a nation. She ran a wide variety of races, including the London Marathon, London Triathlon and Great North Run, and completed a number of cycle challenges, including biking from Rome, Italy to her home in Leeds. As of 2005, Jane raised over £1.25 million for her charity Jane's Appeal (www.janesappeal), which supports various children and cancer charities.

In late 2005, Jane Tomlinson decided that her final challenge would be to undertake a cycle ride across America from the west coast to the east coast. This was to be one of the greatest endurance feats ever attempted by someone with terminal cancer. Jane's aim was to raise her fundraising total to over £1.5 million. The extraordinary nature of the challenge was chosen with care. This was because with each challenge Jane completed, it became apparent that the public would only respond if the feat was viewed as even more remarkable than the last one. For Jane, this meant she had to top the Florida Ironman Triathlon, which comprised a 2.4 mile swim, 112 mile bike and 26.2 mile full marathon run in November 2004.

To make this possible from an organizational perspective, Jane enlisted help from her husband Mike, children's charity SPARKS (one of the benefiting charities of Jane's Appeal), author Ryan Bowd and a group of Leeds Metropolitan University (LMU) students. The latter two were tasked with gaining corporate sponsorship, both in cash and in kind for the ride, developing a corporate identity and developing a media relations plan and press campaign for both UK and US media to raise awareness of Jane's campaign.

The overall campaign objectives set for the communications team of LMU students under the direction of the author fell into three main related areas:

Figure 2.1 Jane on Staten Island

OBJECTIVES

PR

1. Raise awareness of Jane Tomlinson's cycle ride across America in order to raise her fundraising total to over £1.5 million for Jane's chosen charities in the UK and generate additional funds in the US.
2. Plan the PR logistics both in the UK and in the US.
3. Generate media coverage pre-ride, during ride and post-ride.
4. Avoid media fatigue about Jane Tomlinson following previous charity/media activities.

The fourth objective was set as it was a real concern that the ride could suffer from too much media attention in the build up to and early stages of the ride, with the risk that the British public's fickle attention could pass. If that happened, the finish would not capture their attention. Experience had proven to Jane's Appeal that this was one of the key donation periods.

Marketing

5. Find a title partner and raise £50,000 worth of sponsorship and in-kind donations to enable all monies raised to go towards chosen charities.

Identity design

6. Develop a recognizable corporate identity/brand for the ride
7. Make the identity appealing to both the British and American public and media.

There was strong reasoning behind the emphasis on a clear brand identity for this client brief. Once again, it came from an awareness of people's limited attention spans and the risk of donor fatigue. The charity sector is highly competitive, with a profusion of individuals involved in physical challenges and feats of endurance to back their chosen causes. Strong branding was essential to make Jane's personal challenge stand out from the crowd.

PLANNING

Planning began in earnest in January 2006. The communications team was split into three groups; sponsorship and marketing, press communications and brand identity. Weekly meetings were held to update on progress in each area.

BRAND AND IDENTITY CREATION

The brand identity team got to work and came up with a logo that incorporated the Union Jack flag design of Great Britain and the Stars and Stripes flag design of the United States of America set against a map of America. This was done as an attempt

Figure 2.2 Logo

to gain the support of the American public and media; it was deemed vital not to alienate these publics as a proportion of the money raised during the ride would go to an American charity, the Damon Runyon Cancer Research Foundation. It was decided that the name of the ride should be Jane's Ride Across America as it was simple, hard-hitting and explained exactly what Jane was to do. Other names such as From Golden Gate to New York State were explored. Although they were appealing to the riders and team, they were dismissed as they would not resonate with public who were less involved in Jane's efforts.

RAISING THE SUPPORT NECESSARY

The sponsorship and marketing team sent a personally targeted email to the PR departments of large organizations and companies explaining who Jane was, what she was to do and what would potentially be done for the sponsor in return. Those organisations who expressed an interest then received an individually tailored proposal. Such proposals in the end were sent to over 150 organisations. Documents were followed up with face-to-face meetings with seriously interested parties.

Leeds Metropolitan University was soon signed as principal sponsor due to Jane's close associations with the university. LMU had already bestowed an honorary degree on her and its own staff and students were already heavily involved in the fundraising appeal.

Because LMU had recently rebranded and was (and is still) growing its own brand capital in the region and beyond, it was a smart move. With both the regional and national general public, Jane's personal brand could have been viewed as the stronger of the two at the time. It was hoped that the association would deliver clear branding on her clothing across a wide platform of media and that the association would enhance LMU's reputation for being a good corporate citizen.

Further sponsorship was agreed with Adidas Eyewear, Gatorade, Continental Tyres, Yorkshire Bank and M-Power Communications (a satellite phone service provider). The first three of these relationships were struck on the basis and belief that the relationship would deliver a good amount of brand/logo impressions in the general media and that in specialist sport titles it would deliver messaging that would add to the brand's social credentials.

PRESS RELATIONS BY PARTNERSHIP

While this was all progressing, the press communications team and the Tomlinson family planned the media relations strategy for the ride in both the US and the UK.

In the UK, the team were starting from a strong position due to Jane's existing profile and reputation. This was a position that she did not have in the US.

However, fortunately for the team, Jane's media-savvy husband had already thought about this the year before and had laid foundations in the US. These foundations were laid in late 2005 when a partnership for the ride was struck with a US charity, the Damon Runyon Cancer Research Foundation, and Jane travelled to

New York to compete in the world-famous New York marathon. The PR team at the Damon Runyon Cancer Research Foundation arranged for Jane's story to be featured during the marathon and for her to be interviewed live from the course. It was an interview that would hopefully raise funds for them on the day but, more powerfully, would help to build Jane's media profile in the US for when she returned the next summer.

With this in mind, the media strategy for the ride was devised. Communications before the event would focus on the UK. It was decided that with good lead-up prior to the ride, a launch (2 months beforehand at the end of May) would be done to raise awareness of the feat, deliver initial return to sponsors and raise funds for charity. It was decided that the live interviews would be done on consecutive days in London and Leeds as the national television and broadcast media in the UK would only be interested in such a human interest story if they were able to break it before their regional counterparts, who would cover the story the next day due to Jane's regional profile. National and regional print media were provided with copy, images and embargoed interviews in advance of the national media interviews, so that they too were able to run the story on the day of the London launch. Photography for the launch had been done with the regional media and the Press Association for national media distribution the previous week in Leeds. As for copy, the team drafted an extensive media pack to be given to press. This included a launch press release, a quirky yet informative fact sheet about the ride, a biography of the riders, a fact sheet on the partners and charities, a week-by-week itinerary and maps. (See Appendix 2.1 for ride route and interesting facts week-by-week page sample.)

Additionally, prior to the launch, the *Yorkshire Post* and Real Radio were informed of the ride. They immediately expressed an interest in being official media partners. Sky News also agreed a formal partnership which included a documentary of the ride, daily news updates on Sky News Channel, montage summaries of each week's riding shown on the weekend on Sky News Channel and a daily blog by their cameraman, freelance broadcast journalist, rider and friend of Jane, Martyn Hollingworth. Furthermore, the Press Association were approached to provide non-feature copy and images to print media nationally and, where granted, exclusivity of images taken by the author and Mike Tomlinson for distribution beyond media partners and specialist publications such as UK sports publications *220 Triathlon*, *Cycling Weekly*, *Running Fitness* and *Runners* World, which had previously covered Jane's exploits in triathlon, cycling and running. The rationale behind the media partnerships and smaller media list was that despite the risk that they might cause the alienation of some of those media outlets/competitors, the partnerships made it more likely that the relationship would deliver greater depth of coverage and in turn raise greater funds.

This was perhaps one of the greatest strengths of the campaign. Negotiating the various media partnerships and managing the mix was a time-consuming process which called for considerable diplomacy. Fundamentally, though, it can be seen as a specialized branch of stakeholder management, which involves being able to anticipate and fulfil each stakeholder's needs without compromising others. Here, a detailed knowledge of each medium's news values, print and broadcasting timetables and other constraints and requirements enabled communication planners to predict which media opportunities in the forward plan would appeal to each one and pitch that specific stage or event to them. The focus was then on careful stage management to ensure that each medium received what was promised, without impinging upon others. Precedence was given to those who, like Sky TV, held partnership status through their major sponsorship and were media representatives.

Further to this, the Jane's appeal website (www.janesappeal.com) was revamped with a ride-specific version, complete with blog by her husband Mike Tomlinson and her co-riders. It included full ride information, a US and UK donation facility, a media area, interactive ride maps and a discussion area for members of the public to leave messages of support. The website and blog, it was believed, would provide the media with a great source of family and public insight during the ride in a way that would not appear forced or contrived.

For the US launch the Damon Runyon Cancer Research Foundation's PR agency, Fleishman Hillard arranged an interview for Jane with the American breakfast television programme *Today Show* on a US pre-ride exclusive basis in New York the week before the ride commenced in San Francisco. As the programme has a daily reach of over 30 million, the exclusive was deemed more than an acceptable trade-off.

POST-LAUNCH MEDIA

After the high-profile launch a series of follow-up stories were sold to the UK print media. Sizeable breaks were taken between stories to prevent media fatigue about Jane and the ride.

Relationships were also formed with Yorkshire ITV and ITV (ITN) news, which went to the US for the first and last weeks of the ride. ITN arranged for a special feature each week on the lunchtime news, with footage and interviews shot by Jane's son Stephen. These relationships were agreed in ways that would not break the terms or spirit of Sky partnerships.

For the duration of the ride, the Press Association provided a continual feed to the UK national and regional press by sending out news and pictures of Jane's progress. These updates and imagery were sent to the Press Association by a PR team member on the ride.

Throughout the ride, Mike Tomlinson posted a regular blog on the Jane's Appeal website with news of the ride and Jane's condition. This was regularly referred to by national and regional media.

At the end of the ride on the last day, a large photo call with UK and US media was arranged in New York for Jane's finish in Battery Park in the shadow of the Statue of Liberty. Over 30 media outlets attended this alone, irrespective of whether their competition had received exclusive or privileged content.

RESULTS

As a result of this work the following was achieved by the campaign.

Figure 2.3 On the road

PR

In the UK, over £130,000 was raised for Jane's Appeal during the ride. At least a further £120,000 raised after the ride had been executed. This helped to bring Jane's fundraising total to over £1.5 million in the UK. The US charity experienced a noticeable peak in donations after the *Today Show* appearance. However, due to their online donation system, it was not possible to extrapolate an exact amount raised during the ride.

Over 1,200 editorial pieces appeared in both the UK national and regional media and online before, during and after the ride. This was worth approximately £3 million in PR value.

There was more than 100 hours worth of broadcast coverage. This was worth approximately £4 million in advertising value. A significant amount of this was generated as a result of the Sky media partnership, where a Sky News reporter formed part of the riding team and filmed Jane's progression throughout the ride. This saw daily updates on Sky News, weekly montages and an hour-long documentary at the end of the ride, which has aired more than a dozen times on various Sky channels.

Press coverage was all positive. No letters to editors articulating any media fatigue about Jane were published.

Extensive coverage was gained in the US with coverage appearing on the NBC *Today Show*, on the ABC network, in US regional papers and on numerous radio broadcasts. Estimated total PR value was £2.4 million.

Figure 2.4 Ryan Bowd

The campaign raised Jane Tomlinson's profile and she was able set up Jane Tomlinson's Run for All: the Leeds 10k Race in June 2007, which was to be the last fundraising event for Jane's Appeal within her lifetime.

Marketing

More than £50,000 worth of sponsorship was gained to fund the ride. LMU, the title sponsor, received significant coverage in editorial mentions, in branded interviews and on branded clothing that was worn by Jane during the ride. This was worth £2 million of PR value.

During the course of the ride, the website received over 200,000 hits per month, with the majority of donations made online via the site. On average posting on the blog received 20 comments of support per day. Hundreds logged on the final day of the ride.

Identity design

The logo featured heavily in the media and was used as a specific graphic by US and UK television media outlets. It looked very good in print. The Press Association chose an iconic image of Jane wearing a ride logo-branded jacket as the lead picture for launch coverage. This picture featured extensively in the press; several journalists even commented on how effective the ride logo was at communicating the ride concept.

PARTNER RELATIONSHIPS

The success of a logistically-challenging event and sponsorship strategy depends on making and maintaining a wide network of stakeholder relationships. The following feedback to author and campaign manager Ryan Bowd from key partners illustrate their satisfaction with the way in which their respective needs had been met by the campaign:

> Working with Jane's Ride Across America proved to be an excellent venture for us. Commercially we got a great return on investment thanks to the PR team and personally we were proud to support Jane.
>
> Ben Ashlin, Sports Marketing, Adidas Eyewear UK

> Quite simply the PR team were an asset to us and helped to produce some unique and dynamic coverage. . .a pleasure to work with. . .
>
> Dave Harrison YTV, ITV and ITN Ride Across America Coverage Producer

> We were incredibly impressed with the staff, students and whole PR team. In a short period they accomplished an ambitious level of activity.
>
> Without their contribution the ride would not have happened and we would not have raised the amount of money we did for good causes.
>
> I am incredibly grateful for their contribution and dedication.
>
> Jane Tomlinson, CBE

KEY LESSONS LEARNED

Issues identification

- Draw on different expertise to identify issues.

As identified earlier, two key issues faced the campaign planners.

- The crowded and competitive nature of the charity fundraising sector make it hard for any individual or charity to stand out in the eyes of the news media, the public and potential donors.
- Both news media and their users have limited attention spans. Ironically, this poses the risks of media fatigue for fundraisers who have the longest-standing careers and early peaking for media campaigns who cover extended feats of endurance, such as Jane's Ride Across America.

These issues were identified and addressed through the combined expertise of Jane's Appeal and the communications team, highlighting the importance of drawing on both client and practitioner experience at the issues identification stage.

Branding and sponsorship

• Strong branding is important in the charity sector.

A strong visual brand for the event, drawing on Jane's personal brand capital and carefully planned to appeal to audiences in both nations was crucial to differentiating Jane's Ride Across America from the number of other sporting events which raise money for charity. The strong visual impact of the brand was essential to memorability, as well as in securing wide media coverage.

Multiple sponsors = multiple returns

The success of the campaign was founded on a partnership approach with no less than seven overall sponsors, and three media sponsors. Typically for the field of sponsorship, the initial search for these sponsors required a huge amount of research and preparation. With careful negotiation and recording of the different sponsorship rights accorded to each, it was possible to satisfy each of the overall sponsors by delivering what had been promised without compromising the rights of the others. Furthermore, given the separate and distinct agendas and needs of media organizations, sponsorship managers can and should expect to negotiate another wave of sponsorship agreements with media partners. The additional benefits to their clients can be considerable, especially when media coverage is a key channel to awareness and donations for charities.

Media management

• Carefully plan and schedule for an extended event.

Once the risk of early peaking and its negative effect on fundraising ability was identified, the communications team were able to plan a longitudinal approach to media relations, balancing the need to sustain interest in the journey with the risk of media fatigue. Hence, long breaks in UK media coverage were a deliberate part of the strategy. This was in marked contrast to the continuous coverage for which an inexperienced client in this sector might have pressed.

One unusual aspect for forward planning of media relations was that Jane's feat was a journey. As such, it was subject to the occurrences and adventures which happen on the road as opposed to on the route map. Because of this, media management needed to take an iterative planning approach, being open to new events and opportunities while keeping an eye on the overall communications strategy.

- Understand how to negotiate and maintain multiple media partnerships.

The ability to predict the likely interest of multiple news media in an event or series of events was crucial to maximizing media coverage in two continents, and to reaching the maximum number of potential donors. Once again, the knowledge of the risk posed by limited attention spans concentrated the campaign on quality not quantity in terms of desired coverage, and informed the approach taken to negotiating exclusives and partnerships.

EPILOGUE

Jane's Ride Across America was Jane Tomlinson's final personal fundraising achievement. In June 2007, she was able to wave off Jane Tomlinson's Run for All: the Leeds 10k Race, which she and her husband had organized. In the same month, she was nominated for a CBE in the Queen's Birthday Honours. It was an award which was made posthumously to her son after her death on 3 September 2007. Her work continues through Jane's Appeal. Under the guidance of her husband and family, it has now raised £1.8 million for cancer care and research.

The campaign for Jane's Ride Across America has been analyzed and reported in the same way as any successful communications strategy. Ultimately, the PR planners had a unique communications resource which not every campaign can call upon – the determined and charismatic personality of Jane Tomlinson herself. She personified and carried her campaign's message throughout her final feat of endurance and to the end of her life.

Appendix 2.1

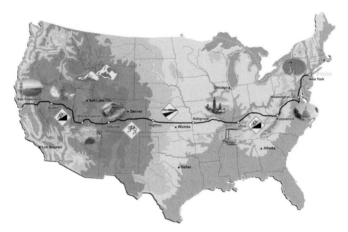

WEEK ONE

Jane's journey begins from San Francisco's Golden Gate Bridge on Saturday 1st July. She will cross the border from California through to Nevada on day four of the ride.

Day 1
Saturday 1st July
Vallejo to Lake Solano Country Park (5miles SW Winters)

Total Distance Travelled 47.5 miles   Cumulative Total 47.5 miles

Day 2
Sunday 2nd July

Winters to Folsom Country Park

Total Distance Travelled 67.5 miles   Cumulative Total 115 miles

Day 3
Monday 3rd July
Folsom to Pollock Pines

Total 43 miles   Cumulative Total 158 miles

Day 4
Tuesday 4th July
Pollock Pines to east of Carson Past

Total Distance Travelled 48 miles   Cumulative Total 206 miles

Day 5
Wednesday 5th July
Carson Pass to Churchill Beach Campground

Total Distance Travelled 92.5 miles   Cumulative Total 298.5 miles

Day 6
Thursday 6th July
Churchill Beach Campground to Cold Springs Station

Total Distance Travelled 79.5 miles   Cumulative Total 378 miles

Day 7
Friday 7th July
Option 1
Cold Springs to Austin (via Mount Airy Summit)
Total Distance Travelled 50 miles

Option 2
Cold Springs to to Austin

Total Distance Travelled 72 miles   Cumulative Total 450 miles

Week 1 Total 450 miles

Fact one - Jane and the team will ride 4214 miles (6780 KM) each, and between
them a combined 12642 miles (20340 KM), equivalent to 3 times the length of
The Great Wall of China.

Fact two - The Golden Gate Bridge in San Francisco has enough steel wires in its cables to circle the earth at the equator 3.5 times. Over 45 million vehicles cross the bridge annually!

Fact three - California is bigger than eighty-five of the smallest nations in the world.

WEEK TWO

Week two sees Jane pass through three states finishing in Colorado. By 14th July she will have covered over 800 miles.

Day 8
Saturday 8th July
no services for 68 miles
Austin to Eureka

Total Distance Travelled 71 miles   Cumulative Total 521 miles

Day 9
Sunday 9th July
no services for 78 miles
Eureka to Ely

Total Distance Travelled 78.5 miles   Cumulative Total 599.5 miles

Day 10
Monday 10th July
no services for 63 miles
Ely to Baker Street Campground

Total Distance Travelled 70.5 miles   Cumulative Total 670 miles

Day 11
Tuesday 11th July
Rest Day 'Great Basin National Park'

Day 12
Wednesday 12th July
no services for 84 miles
Baker to Milford

Total Distance Travelled 84 miles   Cumulative Total 754 miles

FACTS:

1. California is bigger than eighty-five of the smallest nations in the world.
2. Throughout the race 850 litres of water and sports drink will be consumed by the athletes in transition, which in itself is enough to fill 11 full baths.

3. On a bicycle you consume a fiftieth of the oxygen consumed by a motor vehicle, and expel no pollutants.

WEEK THREE

Week three sees Jane pass through Red Canyon Campground finishing in Telluride. By 21st July she will have covered over 65 miles.

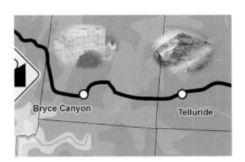

Day 15

Saturday 15th July
Red Canyon Campground to Calf Creek Campground

Total distance travelled 71 miles
Cumulative Total 952 miles

Day 16

Sunday 16th July
Calf Creek Campground to Hanksville

Total distance travelled 96 miles   Cumulative Total 1048 miles

Day 17

Monday 17th July
no services 72 miles
Hanksville to Fry Canyon Lodge

Total distance travelled 73.5 miles   Cumulative Total 1121.5 miles

Day 18

Tuesday 18th July
no services 55 miles
Fry Canyon Lodge to Blanding

Total distance travelled 54.5 miles   Cumulative Total 1176 miles

Day 19

Wednesday 19th July
Blanding to Dolores

Total distance travelled 84miles   Cumulative Total 1260 miles

Day 20
Thursday 20th July
Rest Day 'Mesa Verde National Park'

Day 21
Friday 21st July
Dolores to Telluride

Total distance travelled 65 miles   Cumulative Total 1325 miles

TOTAL DISTANCE TRAVELLED IN WEEK 3: 444 miles

FACTS:

1. 2030 litres of sweat will be lost between them which is enough to fill 254 buckets. This is twice the amount of water the average UK household uses in a week.

2. 2.3255555555 kilowatt hours is the equivalent to 2000 calories

3. Cutting through 1,450 miles of mountains and deserts, the Colorado River supplies water to over 25 million people and helps to irrigate 3.5 million acres of farmland.

WEEK FOUR
Week four sees Jane cycling through Telluride to finish in Dighton covering the distance of 535 miles. By the start of week five she will have cycled 1860 miles in total.

Day 22
Saturday 22nd July
Telluride to Montrose

Total distance travelled 65.5 miles
Cumulative Total 1390.5 miles

Day 23
Sunday 23rd July
Montrose to Gunnison

Total distance travelled 65.5 miles   Cumulative Total 1456 miles

Day 24
Monday 24th July
Gunnison to Cotopaxi

Total distance travelled: 89 miles   Cumulative Total 1545 miles

Day 25
Tuesday 25th July
Cotopaxi to Peublo
Total Distance Travelled: 75 miles   Cumulative Total 1620 miles

Day 26
Wednesday 26th July
Peublo to Haswell

Total distance travelled: 89.5 miles   Cumulative Total 1709 miles

Day 27
Thursday 27th July
Haswell to Tribune

Total distance travelled 80 miles   Cumulative Total 1789.5 miles

Day 28
Friday 28th July
Tribune to Dighton

Total distance travelled 70.5 miles   Cumulative Total 1860 miles

TOTAL DISTANCE TRAVELLED IN WEEK 4: 535 miles

FACTS:

1. Throughout the whole ride Jane will be travelling just 106 miles less than the diameter of the moon.

2. By week 4 Jane has cycled 447 miles more than the distance of planet Pluto's diameter.

3. Jane has now travelled1860 miles in total, which is the same distance as travelling 9 times from London to Liverpool.

WEEK FIVE

Week five sees Jane cycling from Dighton to Ashgrove. Monday July 31st is the half way point for Jane as another 31 days to go before completion

Day 29
Saturday July 29th
Dighton to La Crosse

Total Distance Travelled: 68.5miles
Cumulative Total 1928.5miles

Day 30
Sunday July 30th
La Crosse to Sterling

Total Distance Travelled: 87.5miles
Cumulative Total 2016miles

Day 31
Monday July 31st
Sterling to Newton

Total Distance Travelled: 59.5miles   Cumulative Total 2075.5miles

Day 32
Tuesday August 1st
Newton to Toronto Point Campground

Total Distance Travelled: 99miles   Cumulative Total 2174.5miles

Day 33
Wednesday August 2nd
Toronto to Pittsburg

Total Distance Travelled: 98.5miles   Cumulative Total 2273miles

Day 34
Thursday August 3rd
Rest Day

Day 35
Friday August 4th
Pittsburg to Ashgrove

Total Distance Travelled: 67.5miles   Cumulative Total 2340.5miles

TOTAL DISTANCE TRAVELLED IN WEEK FIVE: 480.5 MILES

FACTS:

1. Jane completed the London marathon in April 2003 and was the first person in the world to have run a marathon on chemotherapy.

2. On a bicycle you can travel up to 1037 kilometres on the energy equivalent to a single litre of petrol.

3. The maximum volume of sweat that a person who has not adapted to a hot climate, such as the American desert, can produce is about one litre per hour.

WEEK SIX

In week six Jane will cycle from Ashgrove to Utica, which is a distance of 505 miles (812.7 km). By the start of week 7 she will have cycle a cumulative total of 2845.5 miles (4579.4 km).

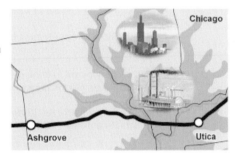

Day 36
Saturday August 5th
Ashgrove to Hartville

Total Distance Travelled: 73miles
Cumulative Total 2413.5miles

Day 37
Sunday August 6th
Hartville to Eminence

Total Distance Travelled: 78.5miles   Cumulative Total 2492miles

Day 38
Monday August 7th
Emimence to Bismarck

Total Distance Travelled: 76miles   Cumulative Total 2568miles

Day 39
Tuesday August 8th
Bismarck to Chester

Total Distance Travelled: 60.5miles   Cumulative Total 2628.5miles

Day 40
Wednesday August 9th
Mississipi Levee Route
Chester to Tunnel Hill

Total Distance Travelled: 85miles   Cumulative Total 2713.5miles

Day 41
Thursday August 10th
Tunnel Hill to Marion

Total Distance Travelled: 61.5miles   Cumulative Total 2775miles

Day 42
Friday August 11th
Marion to Utica

Total Distance Travelled: 70.5miles   Cumulative Total 2845.5miles

TOTAL DISTANCE TRAVELLED IN WEEK SIX: 505 MILES

FACTS:
1. Jane's Ride Across America is the same distance as travelling from Glasgow to London and back again approximately 4_ times.

2. It is very important to drink plenty of fluids when exercising or exposed to high temperatures. Sports drinks contain salts to replace those lost in the sweat.

3. Jane has received over 15 awards for her unique charity efforts, including BBC Sports Personality of the Year award 2002, and a Pride of Britain Award in 2005.

WEEK SEVEN
Week seven will see Jane cycle from Utica, Illinois to Sugar Grove, Illinois. This is going to be the most challenging week for Jane.

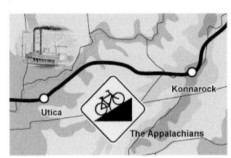

Day 43
Saturday August 12th
Utica to McDaniels

Total distance travelled 53.5miles
Cumulative Total 2899miles

Day 44
Sunday August 13th
McDaniels to Bardstown

Total distance travelled 88miles   Cumulative Total 2987miles

Day 45
Monday August 14th
Bardstown to Berea

Total distance travelled 95.5miles   Cumulative Total 3082.5miles

Day 46
Tuesday August 15th
Berea to Buckhorn

Total distance travelled 73.5miles   Cumulative Total 3156miles

Day 47

Wednesday August 16th
Buckhorn Hindman

Total distance travelled 47.5miles   Cumulative Total 3203.5miles

Day 48
Thursday August 17th
Hindman to Council   27miles

Total distance travelled 95miles   Cumulative Total 3298.5miles

Day 49
Friday August 18th
Council to Sugar Grove

Total distance travelled 83.5miles   Cumulative Total 3382miles

TOTAL MILES WEEK SEVEN: 536.5 MILES

FACTS:
1. Jane has raised £1,120.000 to date for charities including Macmillan Cancer Relief, SPARKS, Damon Runyon Cancer Research and Hannah House.

2. Exercising raises your metabolic rate and your body takes a while to return to its normal state. It continues to function at a higher level that burns an increased number of calories for about two hours after you have stopped exercising.

3. The first race Jane took part in was the UK's 5 km Race for Life in May 2001. Just 5 years on she has taken on the challenge to participate in a bike ride that totals a distance of 6781.8km

WEEK EIGHT
With only 13 days left to go, week eight sees Jane cycling from Sugar Grove to Fredericksberg, which is a distance of 412.5 miles (663.9 km).

Day 50
Saturday August 19th
Sugar Grove to Christiansburg

Total distance travelled 81.5miles
Cumulative Total 3463.5miles

Day 51
Sunday August 20th
Rest Day

Day 52
Monday August 21st
Christiansburg to Buchanan

Total distance travelled 66.5miles   Cumulative Total 3530miles

Day 53
Tuesday August 22nd
Buchanan to Love

Total distance travelled 65miles   Cumulative Total 3595miles

Day 54
Wednesday August 23rd
Love to Palmyra

Total distance travelled 72.5miles   Cumulative Total 3667.5miles

Day 55
Thursday August 24th
Palmyra to Ashland

Total distance travelled 70miles   Cumulative Total 3737.5miles

Day 56
Friday August 25th
Ashland to Fredericksburg

Total distance travelled 57miles   Cumulative Total 3794.5miles

TOTAL MILES WEEK EIGHT: 412.5 MILES

FACTS:
1. To burn a pound of fat you would need to run 33miles.

2. Jane's Ride Across America is 1714 miles longer than her Rome to Home challenge

3. If you cycle for 8 mins this would burn enough calories that are the equivalent of a slice of bread.

WEEK NINE
The final week for Jane comprises of only 6 days, as the bike ride will finish Thursday 31st August in Newark.

Day 57
Saturday August 26th
Fredericksburg to Washington DC

Total Distance Travelled: 90miles
Cumulative Total 3884.5miles

Day 58

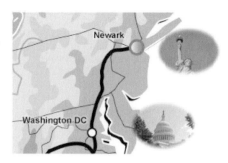

Sunday August 27th
Washington DC to Baltimore

Total Distance Travelled: 70.5miles   Cumulative Total 3955miles

Day 59
Monday August 28th
Baltimore to Marietta

Total Distance Travelled: 76.5miles   Cumulative Total 4031.5miles

Day 60
Tuesday August 29th
Marietta to St Peters

Total Distance Travelled: 63.5miles   Cumulative Total 4095miles

Day 61
Wednesday August 30th
St Peters to Raritan

Total Distance Travelled: 85.5miles   Cumulative Total 4180.5miles

Day 62
Thursday August 31st
Raritan to Newark   33.5miles

Total Distance Travelled: 33.5miles   Cumulative Total 4214miles

TOTAL DISTANCE TRAVELLED IN WEEK NINE: 419 MILES

FACTS:
1. 2000 calories is the equivalent of 0.0644 gallons of gasoline

2. Jane lives in Rothwell, Leeds, and has 3 children

3. Energy burnt by the 3 athletes throughout the course is predicted to be a total of 680400 calories which equates to the same amount of energy needed to light a 60 watt light bulb for just over a month non stop.

3

Kerala, *God's Own Country*

From backwaters to one of the ten paradises on earth

GANGA S. DHANESH

INTRODUCTION

Relationships between organizations and their key publics are built and maintained through building behavioural and symbolic relationships. According to Grunig, what people think of an organization is based on communication about the organization as well as their experience with the organization and others' experience with the organization. Communication can help improve a behavioural relationship between an organization and its publics, but a poor behavioural relationship can thwart attempts to use communication to build a symbolic relationship or to create a positive reputation.[1] In the process of building strategic organization–public relationships, communication plays a tactical supporting role.[2]

This case study illustrates the building of organization–public relationships by initiating both behavioural and symbolic relationships with key publics through an integrated tourism campaign which was launched by the Department of Tourism, Kerala. Kerala is a small state in the south-western corner of India. The campaign eventually catapulted the state from the backwaters of the Indian tourism industry to one of India's best developed tourism destinations, made the travel and tourism industry a major revenue earner for the state and generated employment opportunities for local communities.[3] The campaign also won the Das Golden Stadttor award for its print campaign in 2007.[4]

BACKGROUND

Kerala is endowed with natural beauty – *National Geographic Traveller* magazine described Kerala as 'one of the ten paradises found'[5] – as well as a confluence of native and foreign cultures and human development indicators on par with rich, developed countries.[6] However, it had hitherto been over-shadowed by the Golden Triangle of Indian tourism: the well-known destinations of Delhi, Agra and Jaipur. In

1999, the state tourism sector fetched a mere USD83.22 million in foreign exchange earnings.[7] In order to tap into the potential of the state as an upscale tourist destination and establish it as a major revenue-earner for the state, in the late 1990s the government partnered with the private sector and launched an integrated plan that drew on the synergies among the land, its people and the government. This case study presents key elements of the campaign from 2000 to 2007.

Kerala is wedged between the mountainous Western Ghats on the east and the Arabian Sea on the west. The land lies in humid equatorial tropics and has average annual temperatures from 20.0°C to 27.5°C. Kerala has three geographically distinct regions: the cool mountainous terrain of the eastern highlands, the undulating hills of the central midlands and 360 miles of western coastal plains which are criss-crossed with backwaters. Kerala has around three months of rain every year and receives India's first monsoon, the south-west summer monsoon that blows in from the Arabian Sea. Around 24 per cent of the state is forested and is home to highly diverse flora and fauna[8]. Kerala's agricultural sector produces rice, coconut, tea, coffee, rubber, cashews and spices, including pepper, cardamom, vanilla, cinnamon and nutmeg.[9]

The land, with its bounty of tea and spices, has not only attracted traders from all over Europe for centuries, but it also has assimilated immigrants, including the Dutch, Arab and Portuguese, into its social fabric. Kerala has assimilated descendants of a once-thriving Jewish population in Kochi as well as an enclave of the erstwhile French colony in Mahe.[10] In contemporary Kerala, Christians (19 per cent), Hindus (56.1 per cent) and Muslims (24.7 per cent)[11] live in harmony, for the most part. The society has a vibrant public sphere with high levels of social consciousness and democratic participation, where aware and activist publics actively engage in public debate on social, political, economic and cultural issues.[12]

Moreover, Kerala's human development indices, such as elimination of poverty and provision of education and health care, are on par with European standards. Kerala has one of the highest literacy rates (90.92 per cent) among Indian states. Kerala's healthcare system has been internationally acclaimed, with UNICEF and the World Health Organization designating Kerala the world's first 'baby-friendly state'[13] as an indicator of success in reducing infant death and disease. These indicators are a result of the social reforms initiated by the erstwhile ruling royal families and continued by the democratic governments that followed.[14]

Post-Indian independence, Kerala became the state with the world's first democratically elected communist government. The communist government implemented land and labour reforms which favoured tenants and labourers. The reforms created social equality and spread wealth. However, the socialist ideology embedded in politics and society led to a militant labour culture that resulted in an unfriendly economic environment which was unfavourable for the growth of commerce and heavy industry. On the other hand, the policies and culture that discouraged industry ensured that the natural environment remained relatively unspoilt by the impacts of industry. In the absence of a thriving industrial sector, Kerala is predominantly supported by the service sector and remittances from expatriate Keralites, mostly people who migrated as labourers to the oil-rich, labour-poor countries of the Middle East. Scholars have referred to this economic model of high human development indices coupled with low economic development as the Kerala model of development.[15]

The government is supported by a bureaucracy headed by officers of the elite Central Civil Service cadre, a prestigious pool of public servants selected from all over the country:

> No other State has produced such a long succession of tourism-savvy officials who, unlike their colleagues in other State cadres, have built on their predecessors' achievements. And they are still doing so, supported by a political establishment that had seen the high employment-generation potential of the world's largest industry.[16]

A beautiful verdant land unspoilt by industry, a people who had traditionally welcomed visitors and traders from all over the world, governments that leaned towards socialist principles and a bureaucracy that tended to build upon the work of their predecessors were the choicest ingredients for a perfect tourism recipe. However, in the late 1990s Kerala was literally unknown in the domestic and international tourist circuits.

THE OPPORTUNITY AND THE GOALS

There was ample potential for a vibrant tourism industry created through the synergies among the land, its people and its government. To tap into this opportunity, the key goal of the Department of Tourism, the government department tasked with revamping tourism in the state, was to create a unique positioning for Kerala within the Indian tourism industry as a destination of choice for upmarket tourists while preserving the state's natural environment, cultural artefacts and monuments.[17]

TARGET AUDIENCE

As part of the strategic plan, there was a clear shift in target audience from mass to niche markets that would generate greater revenue and aid in practising sustainable tourism. The newly conceived campaign targeted the 'alert, independent traveller' in search of experiential holidays:

> These travellers seek to touch the heart of Kerala and unveil its soul. They revel in the simplest of pleasures – a lunch on a banana leaf, a refreshing bath in the invigorating monsoon rain or a ride atop a caparisoned elephant.[18]

CAMPAIGN STRATEGY

The campaign strategy planned to achieve its goals primarily by:

- changing the focus of the Department of Tourism from 'selling products to creating experiences, from sightseeing-based tourism to activity-based tourism and from executing transactions to building relationships'[19];

- targeting the upscale segment of the tourist population, who would not only spend more on tourism, but would also tend not to leave an environmental footprint;
- adopting and promoting responsible and sustainable tourism values and practices that would preserve and conserve Kerala's natural and cultural environments.

The campaign was championed by the Department of Tourism in partnership with key stakeholders, such as Kerala Tourism Development Corporation (KTDC), private partners from the hospitality sector, local communities, non-governmental organizations (NGOs), people's representatives and other public sectors such as the railways, airlines and insurance (see Figure 3.1). This strategy was executed through establishing and nurturing relationships with these key stakeholders through open communication and dialogue and by tapping into the synergies among them. The strategy was expected to reposition Kerala's image over time and, in the process, it was expected to deliver mutual benefit to the department and its various stakeholders, including the natural and cultural environments.

THE CAMPAIGN

The two-pronged campaign set out to build behavioural relationships with the stakeholders and target audience by developing policy and infrastructure initiatives while simultaneously building symbolic relationships through the effective use of communication and promotion. The policy and infrastructure initiatives aimed at building behavioural relationships included the following:

1. Kerala Travel Mart Society (KTMS): In 2000, as a first step, the Department of Tourism helped create the KTMS, a public–private sector partnership, to 'become a mechanism for an effective and continuous public/private partnership to facilitate the promotion of tourism in the State of Kerala.'[20] The Society brought together under a common umbrella multiple stakeholders, including airlines, event managers, tour operators, travel agents, travel writers, host communities offering

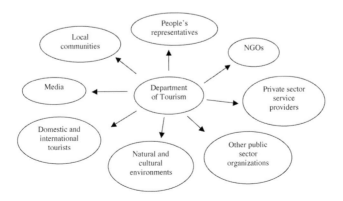

Figure 3.1 The Department of Tourism and its various stakeholders

farm-stays and home-stays, hotels, resorts, houseboat operators, ayurveda centres and organizations promoting eco/adventure/culinary/medical tourism, media, and government agencies.

2. Kerala Travel Mart (KTM): In 2000, KTMS organized the first KTM, the biennial trade event that popularized the new state tourism slogan: 'Kerala, *God's Own Country*'. This event brought together stakeholders from around 50 countries, including India. Successful KTMs have since been conducted in 2002, 2004, 2006 and 2008.

3. Joint ventures for infrastructure upgrades: In 2000, the Kerala Tourism Development Corporation (KTDC), a tourism-related government agency, entered into joint ventures with leading hotel chains, the Oberoi group and the Taj group to develop four hotel properties in Kerala, significantly improving the high-end accommodation infrastructure.

4. Domestic tourism cross-promotional ventures: In 2001, KTDC signed an agreement with the Karnataka State Tourism Development Corporation, the tourism development corporation of another South Indian state, Karnataka, for both parties to work as marketing agents for each other, tapping into the potential of domestic tourism.[21]

5. Rail holidays: KTDC entered into an arrangement with Indian Railways to create a package tour for tourists leaving Mumbai by train for Kochi. An air-conditioned coach attached to the Nethravati Express would carry domestic and international tourists from Mumbai to Kochi every week.[22]

6. Insurance package for tourists: In 2002, the KTDC, in association with United India Insurance Ltd, announced a comprehensive insurance package for tourists visiting Kerala. The package, applicable to tourists coming under three newly launched schemes of KTDC Exclusive Escapades, Age Halt and KTDC Rail Holidays offered compensation to tourists staying in the six premium properties of KTDC for misfortunes that could occur during their stay.[23]

7. Targeted corporate tourism: In 2003, recognizing the growing segment of Indian corporate tourism, Kerala Tourism turned its attention to the domestic market for meetings, incentives, conventions and exhibitions (MICE). It also focused on upgrading MICE infrastructure, including the construction of large convention centres and exhibition venues.[24]

8. Tourism Vision 2025: In 2003, the tourism vision statement was drawn up as a guide for sustainable tourism development:

> To make Kerala, the God's Own Country, an upmarket high quality tourist destination through rational utilisation of resources with focus on integrated development of infrastructure sector conserving and preserving the heritage and environment and enhancing productivity, income, creating employment opportunities, alleviating poverty thereby making tourism the most important sector for the socio-economic development and environment protection of the State.[25]

The tourism vision document was drafted after discussions with stakeholders of the industry, including representatives of the hospitality sector, NGOs and people's representatives.[26]

9. The Kerala Tourism (Conservation and Preservation of Areas) Act, 2005: Kerala became the first state in India to craft a Tourism Conservation, Preservation and Trade Bill, regulate tourism-related activities and ensure the long-term sustainability of the industry.[27]

10. Responsible Tourism (RT) initiatives: Kerala Tourism embraced the tenets of responsible tourism as expounded by the leading international Responsible Tourism group, International Centre for Responsible Tourism at Leeds Metropolitan University, United Kingdom, and conducted a workshop in Kovalam, one of the four destinations chosen to initially implement RT in Kerala. All stakeholders, including tourism industry partners such as tour operators, hoteliers, travel agents, home stay operators, representatives from local governments, people's representatives, NGOs, academics, government officials and media, were invited for the workshop. The Department of Tourism conducted group discussions on economic responsibilities (e.g. buying local produce), social responsibilities (e.g. controlling and selling drugs and sex tourism) and environmental responsibilities (e.g. waste management system, recycling and eco-friendly construction), drew up guidelines based on these discussions and invited hoteliers to come forward to sign the RT initiative.[28]

In addition to these ten policy and infrastructure initiatives that attempted to build behavioural relationships with stakeholders and the target audience, the Department of Tourism built symbolic relationships based on these initiatives. It aimed the promotional campaign at creating positive perceptions about Kerala in the minds of the target audience, including domestic and international travellers. The promotional campaign included print and television advertisements, road shows in foreign and domestic destinations, appointments of brand ambassadors, familiarization tours for travel writers and the creation of tourism-related websites. The following are some of the promotional initiatives undertaken by the Department of Tourism to build symbolic relationships with stakeholders and the target audience:

1. Partnerships with outside agencies: During its inception, the Kerala tourism account was with Mudra, a communications agency. In the mid 1990s, the late Waler Mendis, a copywriter at Mudra, scripted the classic slogan '*God's Own Country*'. When the agency's account director moved to Stark Communications with his team, the account also shifted to Stark. Since then, Stark Communications has played a key role in servicing the account along with three other agencies, each of which handle different areas.[29]

2. Watercolours by God: This award-winning campaign, created in 2000, consisted of a one-minute video clip and print advertisements that highlighted distinct tourism offerings. The campaign was conceptualized and created by the leading Indian cinematographer, Santhosh Sivan. It was later nominated for the Abby award for creative excellence. The 60-second commercial won the Abby silver. Abby awards are given by the Advertising Agencies Association of India (AAAI) for best creative work by ad agencies.[30]

3. State-wide tourism awareness campaign: State-wide tourism awareness campaigns in 2001 were aimed at publics who came in direct contact with tourists,

STEP INTO WATERCOLOURS BY GOD.

And suddenly, you're a poet.

Kumarakom, the heart of backwater country.

In a million shades of green, the endless backwaters meander. Lilies bloom. Lotuses smile. Children play. Coir-women sing. Butterflies dance. Fishes plop. Birds dive. Elephants bathe. The wind whispers. Paddy fields prance. Bullock carts jingle. Ducks glide. Boats sail. Life flows. And suddenly, you're a poet.

kerala
God's Own Country

To holiday in the land chosen by the National Geographic Traveler as one of the ten paradises of the world, write to Kerala Tourism, Park View, Trivandrum 695 033, Kerala. Email: info@keralatourism.org **Toll free infoline: 1-800-425-4747** Fax: 0471-2322279 www.keralatourism.org

Figure 3.2 Step into watercolours by God

such as taxi drivers and tourist police. The campaign stressed the importance of tourism to the state economy and the need to welcome tourists warmly and cordially.[31]

4.   The meetings, incentives, conventions and exhibitions (MICE) campaign: The Department of Tourism's decision to target the corporate tourism segment of

MICE was backed by a 2003 campaign that highlighted Kerala as the perfect place to refresh and revitalize. The campaign presented the corporate sector with large Indian companies and multinationals, including information technology companies and foreign banks and their employees with high purchasing power, with the possibility of a 'working vacation' in Kerala. The campaign's three advertisements (Blossoming Business, Refreshing Agenda and Inspiring Performance) were aimed at introducing and positioning Kerala as a MICE destination. The print campaign, released in trade and business publications and a few general interest magazines, was supported by a direct marketing initiative in key markets that targeted domestic corporations as well as the travel and tourism trade. An information pack detailing the MICE infrastructure was also distributed.[32]

5. Brand ambassadors and publications: Renowned artists such as M F Husain and Yusuf Arakkal were chosen as brand ambassadors. Their paintings and sketches were used to popularize Kerala internationally. A coffee table book, *God's Own Country, a Celebration of Kerala*, with paintings by the famous artist M. F. Husain and text by noted author Shashi Tharoor, was launched in April 2003. Husain's series of 30 paintings, captioned *Kalyanikuttiyude Keralam* (Kalyanikutti's Kerala), was later exhibited in New Delhi. Three tourism brochures promoted various aspects of Kerala Tourism. When Heavens Touch the Earth showed visual snapshots of the monsoons in Kerala. Heal Yourself Here offered information on health tourism and Blossoming Business introduced Kerala as a destination for corporate tourists.[33]

    Yusuf Arakkal's travelogue, *In Touch with my Roots – A Creative Journey through Kerala* published in June 2006 describes Malayalis, as the natives of Kerala are called, and depicts Kerala life in reproductions, drawings, and oil and watercolour paintings.[34]

6. Life in a new light: Research showed that brand fatigue was setting in and the agency's next campaign, in 2005, titled 'Life in a new light' presented Kerala from a fresh perspective and targeted up-market urbanites. The campaign tapped into concepts and motifs from urban life to present Kerala's natural environment in a new light. While the high-rise visual showed rolling hills, the highway visual showed free-flowing backwaters, free of traffic snarls and speeding vehicles and the corporate jungle revealed thick verdant jungles. The campaign comprised six television commercials and a print campaign. It was directed by Santhosh Sivan. Composer and percussionist Taufiq Khureshi created the music.[35]

7. The domestic market: The series of ad films, Life in a new light, was formally launched in Mumbai and Bangalore in 2005. Apart from various international channels, the commercials were also screened in select cinemas across the country, capitalizing on the significance of cinema in the lives of Indians. That same year, the Department of Tourism conducted a series of road shows to promote tourism in the domestic market.

8. Monsoon campaign and Dream season: Kerala's monsoon season has always been its lean season for tourism. Realizing that Kerala was becoming a seasonal destination and going by the Confederation of Indian Industry's report that Kerala had potential for monsoon tourism, the Department of Tourism quietly launched

Figure 3.3 Life in a new light: the highrise visual

Figure 3.4 Life in a new light: the higway visual

campaigns to tap into monsoon tourism. Targeted primarily at domestic tourists from North India and the Middle East, the rains from June to September were positioned as the perfect panacea for the scorching heat of the land of the target audience, as well as a great time to rejuvenate the body with the traditional medicinal treatment of Ayurveda, which is believed to be especially beneficial during the monsoon season. A particularly striking print visual of the monsoon campaign claimed, 'Sometimes it takes water to kindle a fire'.

In 2006, when research showed that Kerala was increasingly being seen as an expensive destination, the Department of Tourism decided to recreate the state's image as a value-for-money destination for all seasons. Building upon the monsoon campaign, the Dream season campaign, extending from April to September, spanned Kerala's summer, monsoon and festival seasons. Targeted at tourists in West Asia and North India, the campaign used a mix of advertising and tourism events to attract visitors. The campaign comprised three print ads that focused on the 'Romance of the rains' and 'Wiping away stress' as well as a radio campaign launched on FM channel Radio Mirchi in the four metro areas of Chennai, Mumbai, Delhi and Bangalore. The events included a monsoon food festival, a music festival and a theatre festival.[36]

The department also worked closely with its partners in the hospitality industry to create special monsoon travel packages priced at rates as low as USD111. The campaign also facilitated interaction between sellers and potential tourists by creating an online presence through a site, www.keralatourism.org/dream season within the Kerala tourism website. Over 135 sellers, such as tour operators and hoteliers, submitted tour packages. Nearly 6,000 buyers visited the site within the first three weeks of its launch.

Figure 3.5 A print advertisement from the monsoon campaign

9. *God's Own Country* works on you: In December 2006, Kerala Tourism launched an experiential campaign that narrated the stories of selected visitors whose lives had been profoundly touched and transformed in some way by Kerala.[37] The creative ideas for the advertisements stemmed from the annual dialogues the agency Stark Communications had with over 1,000 travellers in Kerala. The travellers shared their travel stories with the agency. Five of these stories were chosen for the 2006 campaign. One of these told the story of Serefa Malamati from Greece, whose five-year-old backache was cured by Ayurvedic treatment. Another narrated the tale of Corinne Mathou, from France, who was enthralled by the dance drama Kathakali. She chose to live in Kerala for nine years to learn this art form. Yet another story narrated the search by New Zealanders John and Nicola for the perfect place for their wedding, which took place on the shores of Kerala.

    The initial campaign, in English, ran in Indian and international publications. It later ran in French and German. The campaign also included a strong interactive component on the internet, where travellers were encouraged to share stories of their Kerala travel experience. At the time of writing, over 200 tourists have shared their stories. These stories add to the database for future experiential campaigns. This campaign went on to win the Das Golden Stadttor (The Golden City Gate) awards, which are often referred to as the Oscars of the travel industry, at ITB Berlin for the best print advertising campaign of the year.[38]

10. Participation in trade fairs: The Department of Tourism participated in trade fairs, such as ITB Berlin and WTM London, under their own banner as a separate entity from the Indian tourism department's pavilion, thus reinforcing Kerala's image as

Figure 3.6 God's Own Country works on you: Corinne's tale

Figure 3.7 God's Own Country works on you: the story of a wedding

a unique travel destination within the Indian sub continent. The Department of Tourism participated in national and international trade meets, including national tourism fairs at Bangalore, Chennai, Kolkata and New Delhi, and international travel fairs, such as ATM Dubai, ITB Berlin, PATA Singapore and WTM London.[39]

RESULTS – MUTUAL BENEFITS

These combined efforts to build behavioural and symbolic relationships through developing policy and infrastructure initiatives and simultaneously promoting Kerala tourism through a mix of marketing and public relations campaigns soon paid off. In 2007, more than 500,000 international tourists and over six million domestic tourists visited Kerala. The tourism industry generated revenues of USD 2286.60 million, a 25.27 per cent increase over the previous year. Kerala generates a million employment opportunities directly and indirectly in tourism.[40] Kerala has established its presence in emerging European tourist markets, like Spain, Italy and Russia, apart from traditional Western European markets, such as the United Kingdom, Germany and France. Kerala was one of the few world tourist destinations that could surmount the crises created by the September 11 attacks, the SARS scare and the 2004 tsunami in the Indian Ocean.[41] Growing at an annual rate of 13.31 per cent, the Kerala tourism industry is a major contributor to the state's current economy.

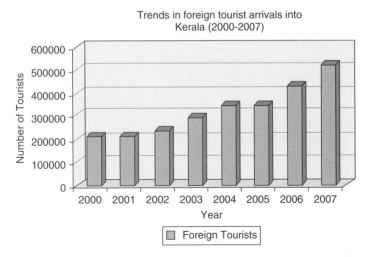

Figure 3.8 Trends in foreign tourist arrivals into Kerala (2000–2007)

Source: http://www.keralatourism.org/tourismstatistics/Microsoft%20Word%20-%20Tourist_statistics_for_Internet.pdf

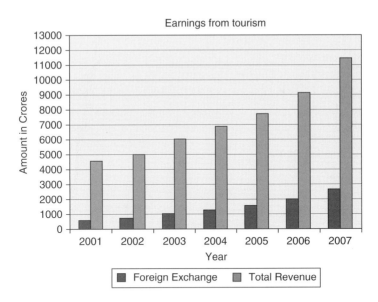

Figure 3.9 Earnings from tourism

Source: http://www.keralatourism.org/tourismstatistics/Microsoft%20Word%20-%20Tourist_statistics_for_Internet.pdf

INTERNATIONAL AWARDS

In addition to meeting the objectives of repositioning Kerala's image as a travel destination, the Department of Tourism's promotional campaigns have bagged many national and international awards, including: [42]

- Das Golden Stadttor award for the Print campaign, ITB Berlin, 2007
- Das Golden Stadttor Award for Best Commercial, 2006
- WTTC Tourism for Tomorrow awards, destination category, 2006 (one of three finalists)
- Pacific Asia Travel Association (PATA) awards:
  - Grand award for Environment, 2006;
  - Gold award for Ecotourism, 2006;
  - Gold award for Publication, 2006;
  - Gold Award for E-Newsletter, 2005;
  - Honourable Mention for Culture, 2005;
  - Gold Award for Culture, 2004;
  - Gold Award for Ecotourism, 2004;
  - Grand Award for Heritage, 2002.

UPDATES

The Department of Tourism has continued with its initiatives, building on prior achievements. In March 2008, Kerala hosted the Second International Conference on Responsible Tourism in Destinations. The conference, attended by academics and representatives from government agencies, NGOs, media and the travel and tourism industry from the state, national and international arena, discussed topics such as local economic development and poverty reduction, taking responsibility for destination sustainability, travel philanthropy and the role of national and local governments.[43]

Giving a further fillip to state tourism, the port town of Kochi, Kerala was chosen as a port of stopover for the 2008/2009 Volvo Ocean Race. This is the only stopover in India. The seven yachts reached Kochi from the previous stopover, Cape Town, before proceeding to Singapore.[44]

LESSONS LEARNED

Building relationships

It is evident from the case study that the Department of Tourism emphasized building and fostering relationships amongst stakeholders by forging multiple partnerships among the various stakeholder groups, such as government agencies, service providers in the private sector, local communities, NGOs, people's representatives, communications agencies and the media. The state played a crucial role by creating favourable policies for infrastructure improvement and destination promotion while regulating the legal environment to protect the natural environs from over-exploitation and to conserve Kerala's cultural artefacts and monuments. The private sector, duly regulated, invested in the tourism sector and generated wealth for businesses, the state and local communities. The involvement of the local communities, NGOs and people's representatives enabled two-way communication and dialogues that not only tied initiatives such as responsible tourism to concepts and ideas from the grassroots, but also enabled acceptance among the participating stakeholders.

Integrated communication campaigns

The favourable policy and infrastructure initiatives went hand-in-hand with the communication campaign that aimed to create a unique positioning and reputation for Kerala tourism. The shift from mass tourism that had attracted counter culture youths to Kerala in the 70s to niche tourism that targeted the more up-market, sophisticated traveller looking for exotic experiences helped in repositioning the state. Starting with the Kerala Travel Mart in 2000 that popularized the slogan '*God's Own Country*', most of the structural initiatives were accompanied by a related communication campaign. For instance, when the state decided to target corporate tourism and worked on up-grading the MICE infrastructure, it also initiated a communication campaign that targeted the corporate buyer. Though each communication campaign went hand-in-hand with a related product initiative, all the campaigns were integrated under the umbrella of '*God's Own Country*', and all the materials spoke the same language, targeting the same customer. Kerala thus executed an integrated communication and promotional plan.

Use of dialogues and multiple models of communication and public relations

In crafting the initiatives that moved the industry forward, the Department of Tourism adopted an open two-way model of communication whereby it elicited the views and opinions of the industry's stakeholders, including NGOs and people's representatives, engaging stakeholders in dialogues and discussions. The open two-way flow of ideas and communication through both direct and mediated channels resulted in initiatives that were sustainable in the long run. This approach was evident both in the drafting of the Tourism Vision statement as well as in the drafting of the RT initiatives. On the other hand, the department engaged in asymmetrical models of communication when it gathered information on its target audiences to better customize the communications campaigns to meet the needs of the target segment. The department also utilized the publicity model and public information models in its communication and awareness campaigns aimed at changing perceptions of Kerala.

Focus on sustainability and harmonious relationships between people and nature

Peterson and Norton[45] stressed the importance of facilitating discourses of sustainability. They noted:

> As human cultures have become increasingly aware of environmental issues and have expressed a desire to participate in the regulatory process, the problem of constructively incorporating public interests has become a central concern for many government agencies, private corporations, and interest groups.
>
> p. 360

Engaging in open dialogues with stakeholders and incorporating issues of public interest into its tourism initiatives have enabled the Department of Tourism to sustain a relatively harmonious relationship between people and the natural environment.

CONCLUSION

The case of *God's Own Country* is not one without issues. The state faces problems of over-development, such as pollution and crowded concrete constructions that sometimes mar the beauty of the landscape. There is also the threat of political and bureaucratic pressures that might harm all that has been done by previous governments who have so far built upon the successes of their predecessors. Despite the threats, the success of the campaign so far has come from tapping into the synergy among the land, its people and the government. The success is based on building and maintaining relationships with multiple partners that bring mutual benefit to all concerned. If this strategy is consistently implemented, the long-term sustainability of *God's Own Country* as one of the ten paradises on Earth might be ensured.

NOTES

1 Grunig, J.E., 'Image and substance: from symbolic to behavioural relationships', *Public Relations Review*, vol. 19, 1993, pp. 121–39.
2 Ledingham, J.A., 'Explicating relationship management as a general theory of public relations', *Journal of Public Relations Research*, vol. 15, 2003, pp. 181–98.
3 India Brand Equity Foundation, 'Investment climate in Kerala', 2008. Online. Available HTTP: <http://www.ibef.org/download/IBEF_KERALA_230608.pdf> (accessed 24 November 2008).
4 Official website of Department of Tourism, Government of Kerala, 'Awards'. Online. Available HTTP: <http://www.keralatourism.org/awards.php> (accessed 24 November 2008).
5 McKibben, B., 'Paradise found: Kerala, India', National Geographic Traveller, October 1999. Online. Available HTTP: <http://www.nationalgeographic.com/media/traveler/kerala.html> (accessed 18 February 2010).
6 Bajpai, N., 'India: towards the millennium development goals', Background paper for Human Development Report, United Nations Development Programme, 2003. Online. Available

HTTP: <http://hdr.undp.org/docs/publications/background_papers/2003/India/India_2003.pdf> (accessed 24 November 2008).

7 Official website of Department of Tourism, Government of Kerala, 'Tourist Statistics 2003'. Online. Available HTTP: <http://www.keralatourism.org/tourismstatistics/TOURIST STATISTICS2003.pdf> (accessed 2 November 2008).

8 Official web portal of Government of Kerala, 'General features'. Online. Available HTTP: < http://www.kerala.gov.in/> (accessed on 24 November 2008).

9 Official web portal of Government of Kerala, 'Economy'. Online. Available HTTP: <http://www.kerala.gov.in/> (accessed on 24 November 2008).

10 Official web portal of Government of Kerala, 'Early history'. Online. Available HTTP: <http://www.kerala.gov.in/> (accessed 24 November 2008).

11 Census of India, 'C Series: social and cultural tables', 2001. Online. Available HTTP: <http://www.censusindia.gov.in/Census_Data_2001/Census_data_finder/C_Series/Population_by_religious_communities.htm> (accessed 24 November 2008).

12 Tharamangalam, J., 'The perils of social development without economic growth: the development debacle of Kerala, India'. Online. Available HTTP: <http://www.infra.kth.se/courses/1H1142/Kerala_Paper_4.pdf> (accessed 24 November 2008).

13 Ramakrishnan, V., 'Indian state wins "baby-friendly" award', BBC News, World Edition, 1 August 2002. Online. Available HTTP: <http://news.bbc.co.uk/2/hi/south_asia/2166677.stm> (accessed 18 February 2010).

14 Tharamangalam, J., op.cit.

15 Tharamangalam, J. (ed.), *Kerala: The Paradoxes of Public Action and Development,* Orient Longman, 2006.

16 Gantzer H. and Gantzer, C., 'The genesis of "God's Own Country"', *The Hindu,* 3 November 2002, para 4. Online. Available HTTP: <http://www.hinduonnet.com/mag/2002/11/03/stories/2002110300730800.htm> (accessed 30 October 2008).

17 Official website of Department of Tourism, Government of Kerala, 'Tourism Vision'. Online. Available HTTP: <http://www.keralatourism.org/tourismvision/VisionIndex.htm> (accessed October 15, 2008).

18 Consumer Superbrands, 2007, p. 107. Online. Available HTTP: <http://www.superbrandsindia.com/images/superbrands_book_2007/Kerala%20Tourism.pdf> (accessed 15 October 2008).

19 Ibid.

20 Kerala Travel Mart, 'The KTM Society', para 2. Online. Available HTTP: <http://www.keralatravelmart.org/htm/the_ktm_society.htm> (accessed 15 October 2008).

21 *The Hindu,* 'KTDC-KSTDC tie-up to boost tourism', 15 December 2001. Online. Available HTTP: <http://hinduonnet.com/2001/12/15/stories/2001121501531400.htm> (accessed 28 October 2008).

22 Ibid.

23 *The Hindu Business Line,* 'KTDC insurance scheme for tourists', 24 January 2002. Online. Available HTTP: <http://www.thehindubusinessline.com/2002/01/24/stories/2002012400600200.htm> (accessed 15 October 2008).

24 Radhakrishnan, S., 'Kerala's MICEtrap', *The Hindu Business Line,* 8 May 2003. Online. Available HTTP: <http://www.thehindubusinessline.com/catalyst/2003/05/08/stories/2003050800120300.htm> (accessed 15 October 2008).

25 Official website of Department of Tourism, Government of Kerala, 'Tourism Vision Statement'. Online. Available HTTP: <http://www.keralatourism.org/tourismvision/VisionIndex.htm> (accessed 12 October 2008).

26 Official web portal of Government of Kerala, 'Tourism Vision 2025'. Online. Available HTTP: <http://www.kerala.gov.in/dept_tourism/initiatives.htm> (accessed 15 October 2008).

27 Official website of Department of Tourism, Government of Kerala, 'Tourism Act'. Online. Available HTTP: <http://www.keralatourism.org/tourismact.php> (accessed 15 October 2008).

28 Official website of Department of Tourism, Government of Kerala, 'Minutes of the Workshop on Responsible Tourism for Kovalam'. Online. Available HTTP: <http://www.keralatourism.org/announcement/RT/kovalam.htm> (accessed 12 October 2008).

29 Bijoy, A.K., 'In the name of God', 15 May 2005. Online. Available HTTP: <http://www.indiantelevision.com/mam/special/y2k5/kertourism.htm> (accessed 15 October 2008).

30 Superbrands, op. cit., p.107.

31 Official web portal of Government of Kerala, 'Launching of Statewide Tourism Awareness Campaign'. Online. Available HTTP: <http://www.kerala.gov.in/dept_tourism/initiatives.htm> (accessed 12 October 2008).

32 Radhakrishnan, S., op.cit.

33 *The Hindu Business Line*, 'Husain, Tharoor team up to sell Kerala to tourists', 12 April 2003. Online. Available HTTP: <http://www.thehindubusinessline.com/2003/04/12/stories/2003041200321700.htm> (accessed 15 October 15 2008).

34 Arakkal, Y., *In Touch With My Roots-A Creative Journey through Kerala*, India: Penguin Books, 2006.

35 Bijoy, A. K., op. cit.

36 Radhakrishnan, S., 'Kerala Tourism's new "monsoon campaign"', *The Hindu Business Line,* 23 January 2006. Online. Available HTTP: <http://www.thehindubusinessline.com/2006/01/24/stories/2006012402140800.htm> (accessed 15 October 2008).

37 Mathrubhoomi Travel and Tourism, 'Travel and Tourism News', 17 June 2008. Online. Available HTTP: <http://www.mathrubhumi.com/travelandtourism/php/showNews.php?news_id=12100&link_id=14> (accessed 18 November 2008).

38 Radhakrishnan, S., 'Tales of a traveller', *The Hindu Business Line,* 05 April 2007. Online. Available HTTP: <http://thehindubusinessline.com/catalyst/2007/04/05/stories/2007040500130300.htm> (accessed 24 November 2008).

39 Official web portal of Government of Kerala, 'Stress on public – private partnership in promotion'. Online. Available HTTP: <http://www.kerala.gov.in/dept_tourism/initiatives.htm> (accessed 12 October 2008).

40 Official website of Department of Tourism, Government of Kerala, 'Tourist Statistics 2007'. Online. Available HTTP: <http://www.keralatourism.org/tourismstatistics/Microsoft%20Word%20-%20Tourist_statistics_for_Internet.pdf> (accessed 12 October 2008).

41 Superbrands, op. cit. p.106.

42 Official website of Department of Tourism, Government of Kerala, 'Awards'. Online. Available HTTP: <http://www.keralatourism.org/awards.php> (accessed 12 Oct 2008).

43 Official website of Department of Tourism, Government of Kerala, 'Second International Conference on Responsible Tourism in Kerala'. Online. Available HTTP: <http://www.keralatourism.org/news/172/second-international-conference-on-responsible-tourism-in-kerala.php?issueid=172> (accessed 15 October 2008).

44 Kumar, V.S., 'Volvo ocean race: Kochi exempted from paying entry fee', *The Hindu Business Line,* 27 February 2008. Online. Available HTTP: <http://www.thehindubusinessline.com/2008/02/27/stories/2008022750831100.htm> (accessed 02 November 2008).

45 Peterson, T.R. and Norton, T., 'Discourses of sustainability in today's public sphere', In S. May, G. Cheney and J. Roper (eds), *The Debate over Corporate Social Responsibility,* New York: Oxford University Press, 2007, pp.351–64, p. 360.

4

LG Mobile

Utilizing the blogosphere to increase buzz and drive positive sentiment of mobile phones

RONNIE BROWN

INTRODUCTION

LG Mobile is one of the many divisions of LG, the Korean-based conglomerate that has over 130 subsidiaries based all around the globe. LG Mobile is the largest division within LG Electronics and is the world's third largest manufacturer of mobile handsets.

In 2007 LG was a relative recent entrant into the European market and very much a challenger brand. They create sleek and stylish phones that appeal to a design-conscious consumer. While their phones are technically proficient, it is the way they look and feel that are the key selling points.

In August 2007, it faced the following marketing challenges in Europe:

- The mobile handset market was both mature and highly competitive. Samsung, Sony Ericsson and Nokia were ahead of LG in most major European markets.
- LG-aided awareness was comparatively low among consumers. Unaided awareness and consideration at the point of purchase was also low.
- LG Mobile brand perception in the eyes of consumers was neutral.
- LG Mobile did not have the marketing resources to compete directly with the other top handset manufacturers.
- Major new handsets were released nearly exclusively in spring and autumn.

The overall challenge was for LG is to build awareness of its products to drive consideration (and sales), but on a much smaller budget than the competitors. It simply did not have the resources to, for example, try and match Nokia's media spend. Essentially, it had to think smarter and act differently, choosing its media and picking battles where it knew it had a good chance of cutting through to its target consumer.

At this point, and with this brief, LG engaged with Outside Line, a specialist in digital communications, to work on a long-term strategy that addressed these issues from an online perspective.

RESEARCH

Through their own research and segmentation LG had identified a large period of consideration online in the purchase cycle of a mobile phone in its key consumer target group. They called this group 'premium seekers'.

To take a somewhat simplistic view of the purchase cycle, awareness was created by a mixture of traditional media spend (e.g. advertising, PR, etc.), channel activity and word of mouth (WOM). This awareness then drove consumers online where they looked at specifications, compared features and checked review sites, blogs and other User Generated Content (UGC) sites to ascertain a balanced view of and consensus on a product. It was at this stage that they narrow their choice to a few products and, in general, go to the store to see the products demonstrated and be guided (to some extent) by the in-store staff.

This consideration stage was where our work was to be focused. With major review sites already well serviced by the retained PR agency and news sites tending to be more factual than opinionated, we turned our attention to what is termed 'social media'.

We knew from research then and since[1] that consumers were increasingly turning to other consumers online for honest appraisals of products. This could be seen in A. G. Lafley's comments that[2] consumers:

- are less trusting and less responsive to brand messages;
- are more networked than ever;
- have the desire and means to create and distribute content.

Technology, specifically the internet, continues to drive the above trends. The following factors are all becoming second nature to today's consumers:

- the widespread adoption of broadband;
- free online services that allow content creation (e.g. Blogger, YouTube, Flickr, etc.);
- collaborative sites (e.g. Wikipedia);
- information sharing via social bookmarking sites (e.g. Digg, del.ico.us, etc.);
- discussion of opinions on blogs and forums;
- creation and maintenance of relationships through Facebook, MySpace and Bebo.

Within these trends, the rise of blogs has been tremendous in the last few years. In March 2003 there were no blogs at all; by March 2004 there were two million, March 2005 eight million and there are now around 133 million blogs.[3]

It might be helpful at this point to define what we mean by a blog:

A blog is a web site, usually maintained by an individual with regular entries of commentary, descriptions of events, or other material such as graphics or video. Entries are commonly displayed in reverse-chronological order. Many blogs provide commentary or news on a particular subject; others function as more personal online diaries. A typical blog combines text, images, and links to other blogs, Web pages, and other media related to its topic. The ability for readers to leave comments in an interactive format is an important part of many blogs.[4]

The differences between a blog and more traditional media are a blog is self published, spontaneous and conversational (i.e. talking with the audience). Whereas traditional media is owned, scheduled and communicates in one direction (i.e. talking at the audience).

From our own experience we knew that a blogger tends to be:

- openly vocal, with a larger than average ego;
- not constrained by traditional editorial policies;
- often not commercially motivated;
- media- and technologiy-savvy;
- an expert in their chosen field of writing;
- able to influence a loyal and informed readership.

After some in-house research into the activities of Nokia, Sony Ericsson, Samsung and Motorola, we discovered that none of these competitors were engaging with as a media channel. We researched the following questions of the competitor brands:

- Does [competitor brand] have a blog?
- Does [competitor brand] participate actively in the blogosphere by commenting or any other activity?
- Does [competitor brand] send phones to bloggers to review?
- Does [competitor brand] invite bloggers to briefings or run events specifically for bloggers?
- Is [competitor brand] involved in social media in any form?
- Does [competitor brand] involve bloggers in product development or any other form of official feedback?

In nearly all cases the answer was 'no'.

It is worth noting that the volume and sentiment of online debate has been proven to be a key indicator in future sales and market share. Statistical models are built to forecast this.[5]

In summary, we had a medium (i.e. blogs) that was growing in volume and influence and was increasingly read and trusted by the target audience during a critical stage of the purchase cycle. Additionally, there was little to no activity from the competitors, so there was a clearly defined opportunity to engage with the medium in order to drive consideration (and so sales) of LG products.

GOALS AND OBJECTIVES

Primarily, the objective was to increase consideration of LG products to parity with its competitors by:

- increasing the online buzz around its products;
- creating positive sentiment online towards its products.

Secondarily, to further bolster LG's brand promise of stylish design backed by innovative technology.

TARGET AUDIENCES

LG's primary audience segment was what they deem to be 'premium seekers'. These individuals were roughly 20 per cent of their customer base and were the main focus of their marketing activity. They could be characterized as:

- professional / managerial with an above average income and aged in their 30–40s;
- wanting all the latest features on their mobile but unwilling to compromise on style and design;
- doing a tremendous amount of pre-purchase, mostly, if not exclusively on the Internet.

In order to reach this audience, the primary focus of the strategy was to influence the formers of opinion, targeting the top strata illustrated in Figure 4.1 and allowing LG-related information to disseminate from a trusted source to those below them in the hierarchy.

We saw bloggers as the key to this strategy. Bloggers in the mobile phone sector are of primary importance. However, we also saw those in the areas of fashion, design, gadget, technology and innovation blogs all played a role, as these five were key brand sectors for LG.

Being such a new channel, blogs and bloggers were not as well or as thoroughly researched as other media. Technorati's State of the Blogosphere[6] research is still

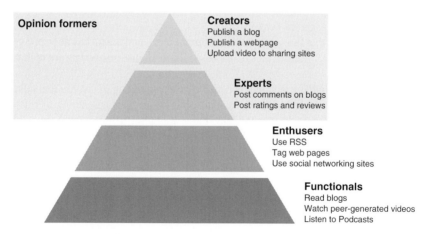

Figure 4.1 Key target audience

generally deemed to be the annual benchmark for the media. It gave the following portrait of the average blogger:

- male (73 per cent in Europe);
- employed;
- educated to at least degree level;
- married or living with a partner;
- has been blogging for nearly three years;
- invests no money in his blog and makes no money from it.

In 2008, when asked 'Why do you blog?' in this survey, the bloggers answers were those summarized in Figure 4.2.

When asked 'What do you blog about?' the responses were those summarized in Figure 4.3.

Further evidence on discussions about brands was also found, as illustrated in Figure 4.4.

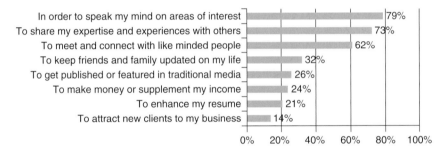

Figure 4.2 Survey response to 'Why do you blog?'

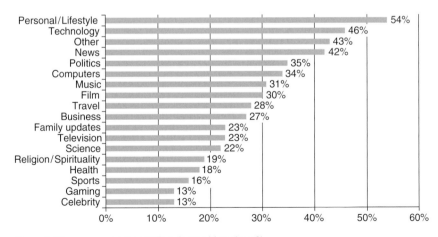

Figure 4.3 Survey response to 'What do you blog about?'

Do you talk about products or brands on your blog?	Frequently	Occasionaly	Never
I post product or brand reviews	37%	45%	18%
I post about brands that I love (or hate)	41	48	11
I blog about company information or gossip that I hear about	31	32	37
I blog about some of my every-day experiences in stores or with customer care	34	45	21

Figure 4.4 Survey response on brands

So, to summarize the above, and the rest of the research, bloggers were characterized as:

- expressive, creative, explorative, experimental and willing to try new things;
- social (i.e. they like to connect, meet and share with others);
- very media- and technology-savvy (i.e. at the forefront of trends, particularly online);
- not usually commercially motivated and independent in thought;
- not a homogenous group (i.e. they are of any race, class, gender, they reflect their community but they do have common needs);
- connected via several other social media areas;
- open to a dialogue with brands;
- not constrained by editorial policies.

COMMUNICATION STRATEGY

In order to shape the communications strategy we asked ourselves one question:

How do you have a credible, long-term and influential relationship with a blogger when product release schedules mean there may be little to say for long periods of the year?

Our answer was simplistic and succinct:

You become part of the blogosphere and join in the existing conversations.

A direct product-centred approach to bloggers may have worked in the short-term if shaped correctly. However, in our experience, better long-term returns were to be gained by:

- demonstrating knowledge of the media and subject matter;
- participating actively, within the community building trust and credibility over time.

By joining in and acting like a regular blogger, LG was deemed authentic and had the right to participate and influence the blogging community from within.

Additionally, by joining in the existing conversations, we were able to fill the content gaps between product releases by keeping in contact with bloggers through commenting on their posts.

We believed this was the correct approach for LG as it:

- created a meaningful, credible and influential relationship with online communities;
- differentiated through active participation (i.e. competition were passive and passionless);
- gave immediate scale and reason to contact by tapping into existing community networks and conversations;
- created a new channel for activating existing, or creating new, brand experiences;
- aided search visibility through the volume of blogs and links;
- propagated LG's brand and ethos beyond just the products.

THE CAMPAIGN

The main aim of the tactical application of the campaign was to create an LG persona online as if LG were a regular member of the blogging community. This persona was completely overt and transparent with regards to our motives. This is not only good practice but also a legal requirement.

The campaign had several distinct but inter-linked phases that are detailed below.

The blog

The first stage of joining the blogosphere as a blogger was to create and manage your own blog, so this is where we started for LG. The blog acted as the central and key property throughout the campaign.

So that the blog looked and felt authentic, we used WordPress, one of the most common blogging tools, to create it. We kept to the usual terminology and structure so as to assimilate the LG blog with other blogs.[7] Factors such as content layout, text treatment and the features (e.g. archive, recent posts, link roll, tag cloud, comments, RSS, email alerts, etc.) were shown in the standard manner on the blog. Reciprocal links were arranged with other relevant LG websites and included in the blog's link roll.

As far as editorial policy, we settled on four key areas to write about: design, technology, innovation and style. These are key brand attributes for LG. Therefore, they would allow us the flexibility to add further products while aiding the brand by reinforcing the attributes to readers.

An 'about us' section was included from the outset so as to state our positioning on why we were there and what our aims were. This initial statement, with its transparency of motives, is essential as a stake in the ground for all who visited the blog.

When the blog first went live, we posted once a day. These posts were roughly 4:1 non-LG- to LG-related content so as to position the persona as a community member rather than as blatant one-way marketing. This was essential in winning trust from the community. The non-LG content continues to be a mixture of posts we create and stories from other blogs upon which LG have a view.

After posting for a few weeks and having gained some standing in the community, we introduced sections for the products themselves and we became a little more overt in our marketing of LG products.

As posts were made to the blog, readers posed questions and made comments. We answered questions where we could – we had regular briefings and training on the major LG products – or referred readers to LG for more detailed or technical enquiries. We accepted negative comments (and countered them where appropriate) and allowed the debate to flow freely and naturally, only intervening where legal boundaries were crossed.

The outreach campaign

This stage of the campaign involved us commenting as LG on the blogs of those we wished to influence, having a view on their content as a regular blogger would. The first stage of this was to draw up the list of bloggers that we deemed to be influential within the fields of design, technology, innovation and style and have also posted content relevant to mobile phones.

We used our own database and several freely available tools (e.g. Google, Technorati, etc.) to research blogs in this area. We then applied the following four criteria to determine the influence of each blog:

1. Reach: How many people read or subscribed to the blog? This could be ascertained from published readership/subscription figures or a complex equation based on several factors to calculate unique users per month.
2. Relevance: How relevant was the content of the media and the demographic of the readership to LG's target audience? The better the fit the greater the potential influence.
3. Expertise: How many times was the blog referenced by its peers online or offline? The greater the expertise in the field the greater the potential influence.
4. Activity: Was there a high level of commenting and debate on the blog? Also, how active and connected was the blogger? That is, were they a member of a social network like Facebook or have an account on Twitter, Flickr, YouTube etc.? The greater the activity on the medium and the more connected it was to other social media, the greater the potential influence.

Once we came to an agreement with the client on the above we began the next stage. This was to start commenting as LG on the target list of blogs in order to introduce ourselves, win credibility, build relationships and finally influence the debate.

To get to this status in the community took time and considerable effort. Theoretically, how this was achieved is demonstrated in the three stages of community involvement:

1. Newbie: When LG entered the blogging community the existing members viewed them, at best, with scepticism or, at worst, as an irritant. They were suspicious of LG's motives and stand-offish. By participating in a conversational and open manner we laid the foundations for the LG persona within the community.

2. Conversationalist: After a while posting and commenting, LG developed a persona. This became established slowly and through online interaction bloggers started to share values and history with LG. It became obvious we had some supporters at this stage and we looked to develop these relationships by using a more familiar tone and approach with them.

3. Community member: At this stage, LG was a known and trusted member of the community. LG was able to participate fully, understand the group dynamics and maybe even to shape the debate's direction. Having earned the right to be in the community we could now more openly influence and utilized more overt marketing in relation to products and brand.

It was essential to the success of the campaign that we were given time to establish LG's presence within the blogging community. The entire campaign could have been undermined if these stages were bypassed or shortcut.

Figure 4.5 captures the process of commenting and its effects during the newbie/conversationalist stage:

We chose to comment on a post on a target blog if it coincided with the four key attributes (i.e. design, innovation, technology and style) and if the content itself was something that LG could take a view on. (See the next section on rules of engagement for the full criteria.) When commenting as LG, we always linked back to our own blog to authenticate the comment as coming from LG. This helped readers find our blog and had positive effects on search engine results by increasing link volume and equity.

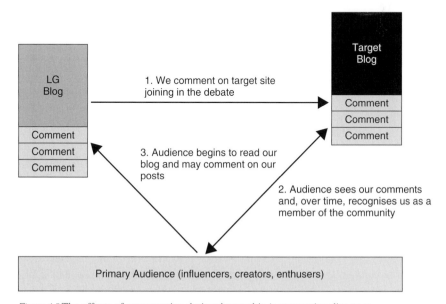

Figure 4.5 The effects of commenting during the newbie/conversationalist stage

Our participation was not limited to merely making one comment and leaving. We acted as a regular community member and engaged in all debate around our topic and all conversations were managed to a natural conclusion. If we were asked direct questions or asked to comment in any way then we acted as a regular community member and responded accordingly.

This period of relationship building lasted around eight weeks as both the bloggers and their readers got to know us via our comments, our conversations and the content on our own blog. At this point, we were deemed a community member and were therefore viewed as authentic. We were able to leverage our credibility and finally be more overt in our marketing efforts.

Rules of engagement

As we were acting as LG online, it was crucial that the persona we created and maintained:

- was aligned with brand values;
- demonstrated an understanding of the media;
- was credible to the community in which we operated.

It was also paramount that we had procedures to deal with red flag-type issues (i.e. those to which LG would prefer we refer to them for a response) and for crisis management.

We drew together these various elements into what we called our 'rules of engagement', which covered subjects such as:

- how we engaged in debate – our philosophy, media choices and topics;
- language used – defining the tone and the more technical aspects of the language we used;
- blog moderation – rules for encouraging debate on the blog while keeping on brand and within legal bounds;
- negative WOM – if and how to dealt with criticism and aggression;
- competitors – how we talked about competitor products and brands;
- mechanics of the LG Persona – what we were called, our names, email addresses, etc.;
- synchronization of information – contacts at LG for questions, placement on distribution lists for product or brand information, definition of issues for escalation, crisis management or major incident briefing, contacts for out of hours issues, etc.

Product reviews

After entering into conversations and building relationships over a number of weeks the next stage of the campaign was to send phones to the bloggers for them to keep, use and hopefully review on their blog.

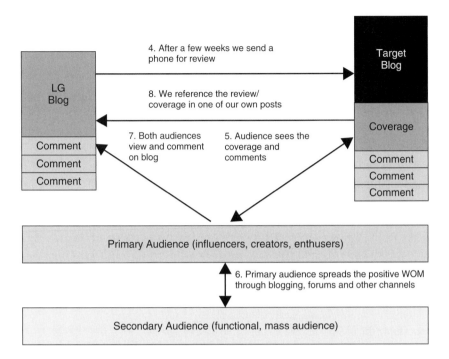

Figure 4.6 The review process and its effects

We sent the phones to the bloggers and followed up with an email stating that they were under no obligation to publish a review, but if they felt they wanted to, assets to support a review (e.g. pictures, specifications, video, etc.) would be provided.

The review itself and the effect this had on the audiences are illustrated in Figure 4.6.

Events

Viewty was the first phone release we supported, in October 2007. We sent this phone out to the bloggers for review. However, for each subsequent phone launched we held an event designed specifically for bloggers. These events included a briefing on the product, a demonstration, questions and answers and then informal discussions between the bloggers and relevant LG staff. The informal discussion was the most important part for the bloggers as it sates their desire to connect, share experiences and talk.

The events were filmed. We also conducted interviews with bloggers at the event to obtain their first impressions of the phone. This footage was then uploaded to YouTube and other video UGC sites shortly afterwards.

Holding an event had several benefits over simply sending a phone to the bloggers. These events:

- deepened the existing relationships with the bloggers;
- created additional positive WOM around the phone ahead of release;

- provided us with immediate feedback on the phone from a tech- and style-savvy audience;
- opened a dialogue with bloggers as to how we could further collaborate in the future.

It is worth noting that after the first event, where we physically met the bloggers, the relationship we had with them became much stronger and closer in every case, showing that there is nothing more powerful than a one-to-one, in-person conversation.

Supporting channels

As our strategy was to act as a regular member of the blogging community we also embraced the other media that bloggers would routinely utilize. We created official LG accounts with the following:

- YouTube: We uploaded content (e.g. product videos, TV adverts, etc.) provided by LG. But we also used it to highlight video that we created. This was usually footage from an event or, in the case of some phones, consumer friendly how-to guides covering the basic features of the phone that we filmed.
- Flickr: We used this photo-sharing site to upload all official LG photos of products. Many of the LG phones have exceptional cameras so we uploaded several pictures taken with the phone to demonstrating the various features and modes. Finally, we used the search facility to locate photos taken with the phone that we liked or were good examples of the specific features of the phone's camera, and we highlighted these in our channel and sometimes on the blog.
- Twitter: This micro-blogging platform was used to highlight our blog posts and other actions between postings. We followed our bloggers' tweets and are followed by others.
- Facebook: We created a fan page for LG Mobile and for the individual phones. The fan pages contained a mixture of content from all the other media we used (e.g. the blog, YouTube, Flickr, etc.). By becoming a fan, a user gained access to additional content. This allowed us to send them messages updating them on the latest news from LG on the specific subject area of the fan page.

All of the above were featured on the blog and, where appropriate, cross-promoted in each of the other media.

RESULTS / EVALUATION

Setting the key performance indicators (KPIs)

There were several hurdles to overcome when setting (KPIs) for an innovative campaign such as this as we are working in a medium that has few agreed or published metrics and its innovative nature means there are few existing campaigns from which to draw parallels.

We used the same KPIs for each of the products we have supported since beginning the campaign. These tie directly back into the objectives and were:

- Share of buzz: The share of buzz indicated how effective the campaign had been at getting LG products talked about online. In other words, the occurrences of the product name within blogs, forums and news sites. Although this metric will include coverage created via other media (e.g. TV, PR, etc.) it was a good overall measure of the amount of online conversation that concerned the products. Our rule was that the LG product should be at least comparable to its immediate competitors. These competitive products were agreed on a case-by-case basis.
- Share of influence: The share of influence took the buzz and weighted the voices (e.g. blogs, forums, news sites, etc.) within the buzz by which voice had the most topical influence. Not all online voices are equal so we attempted to measure how effective we were at engaging with the most influential of them. We used citation indexing as our methodology for determining influence. Again, the LG product should be at least comparable to its immediate competitors, which were agreed on a case-by-case basis.
- Sentiment: The sentiment measured the how the buzz around a term was categorized (i.e. very positive, positive, neutral/questioning, negative or very negative). We achieved this by reading the context in which the term was used and automatically categorizing it. We required the LG product to have a positive overall sentiment and gain, be at least comparable to its immediate competitors.

We used a third-party tool, Influence Monitor by Onalytica, to measure these three key metrics. This gave an independent view of campaign performance and also aided us in several other areas, such as determining new sources of influence and more brand-based monitoring.

You will notice that two seemingly obvious metrics were missing from our KPIs: the amount of traffic to the blog and the coverage gained from the reviews. While they were important – and we did measure them – the three above are the ones that truly measure buzz and drive consideration so they were kept as primary measures.

Additionally we measured and reported on:

- blog traffic;
- review and other blog coverage (e.g.number of pieces and estimated views);
- number of inward links to the blog;
- views of videos via YouTube and other UGC sites;
- number of fans on Facebook;
- numbers followed and following in Twitter;
- Technorati authority.

Results

As we ran campaigns for several products, we will show one example, the LG Secret mobile phone, against its direct competitor phones. The direct competitors were the Nokia N96, Samsung Soul and the Sony Ericsson C905.

Share of buzz

Over the period of the campaign, the Secret had a 25 per cent share of buzz. This was above both the Samsung Soul and Sony Ericsson C902, which both had much larger campaigns (in budget and scope) running at similar times. Nokia dominates proceedings, confirming its status as number one in the UK (with the N82 handset).

What this demonstrated is that on a much smaller investment, LG was able to get more online mentions of this particular product than all but one of its direct competitors (see Figure 4.7 for a comparative summary).

Share of influence

Not all websites are equal in influence so when factoring this in and weighting the results accordingly Secret maintained its share of the more influential sites. In fact the picture remained roughly the same across the competitive landscape, showing that all competitors are equally good at targeting influential online media.

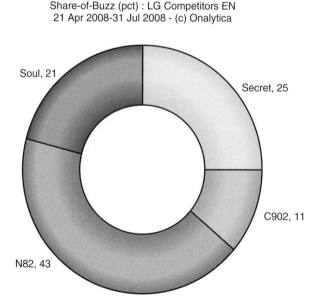

Share-of-Buzz (pct) : LG Competitors EN
21 Apr 2008-31 Jul 2008 - (c) Onalytica

Soul, 21

Secret, 25

C902, 11

N82, 43

Figure 4.7 Comparison of share of online voice for LG Secret

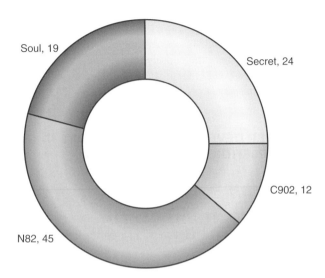

Share-of-Influence (pct) : LG Competitors EN
21 Apr 2008-31 Jul 2008 - (c) Onalytica

Soul, 19

Secret, 24

C902, 12

N82, 45

Figure 4.8 Comparison of weighted share of online voice for LG Secret

Sentiment

The sentiment measured how positive or negative the buzz was around the products. Secret performs very well with an overall positive sentiment of 89, which is second to the Soul's sentiment of 98. It is worth noting that although N82 created the most buzz and had the largest share of influential sites, its sentiment is 40, which is less than

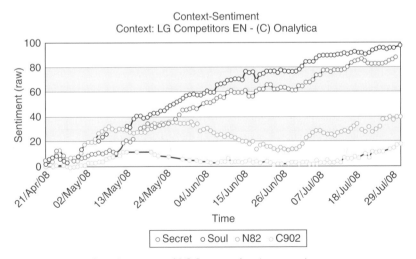

Context-Sentiment
Context: LG Competitors EN - (C) Onalytica

Figure 4.9 Measure of sentiment toward LG Secret and main competitors

half that of Soul and Secret. This shows that it had not been as positively received as the Soul and Secret. C902 lagged a long way behind with a sentiment of 18.

The launch event held for the phone and subsequent reviews created 45 pieces of coverage from our target lists of blogs with a combined reach of 2.4 million users. The official videos and those created by us gained over 300,000 views on YouTube.

While we are unable to share the consideration figures, you can gauge from the above performance against competitors that the campaign had a significant impact here and on sales of handsets.

UPDATE : FURTHER DEVELOPMENTS THAT HAVE TAKEN PLACE SINCE THE COMPLETION OF THE CAMPAIGN

Initially, the campaign was focused in UK, France and Germany (starting in September 2007). After demonstrating success over the first six months, the same format was applied in Spain and Italy in May 2008. Other countries continue to look at the model to see how it can be applied to their particular products and specific market requirements.

As well as expanding geographically, the focus of the blogs and outreach campaign quickly moved beyond mobiles and into other products that LG manufactures where consideration online can be improved. Televisions and other audio-visual (AV) products were an obvious next step; this has been rolled out in several countries. Although it is worth noting that, from our research in the UK, blogs were not such an influential medium with regard to the purchase of AV equipment as forums are. The campaigns were adapted in each country to reflect differing purchase cycles, audiences and media channels.

LESSONS LEARNED: THE LONG-TERM IMPLICATIONS

One of major lessons we learned from the campaign is that the client company has to be both open and in full support of the idea of engaging online in a medium where they do not have complete control of the message. The understanding, at the highest level of the company, that control of the message has been ceded to someone (i.e. a blogger) who is independent, vocal and cannot be manipulated, is absolutely crucial. Luckily with LG we had understanding. However, with many other clients this is a source of contention or it requires a great deal of education within the company.

By putting this campaign into practice we invited debate on products and services on the blog and in many other areas. By definition, those who have an issue tend to be more vocal. Therefore, both the agency and the client need to understand how to deal with complaints and have an open channel of communication to deal with these complaints and questions.

The most influential blogs for the audience may not necessarily reside within the country where the campaign is running. The consumer on the internet deals in language, not necessarily country boundaries. This has implications for the campaign and client. For example, Engadget is a very large gadget blog based in the US. As we could only target UK-based blogs for the UK campaign we could not include it. However, the UK readership of Engadget was ten times the size of the largest UK based blog and was the most influential over a UK audience. In this instance we had to make a case to include a site that traditionally falls under the US client's remit in our UK campaign. Similar issues were raised with Spanish-language blogs from South America being included in the Spanish campaign.

With so many different media and supporting channels it was essential that we integrated and cross-promoted at every opportunity (e.g. featuring the YouTube channel in Facebook, publishing our blog posts in Twitter and using Flickr pictures on the blog). This tying together of channels enabled consumers to have a rich experience and be led through our other properties, whatever their entry point. Furthermore, aligning the campaign with the client's existing activity gives tremendous opportunities for synergy.

One trend that we have noticed since beginning of the campaign in September 2007 is the blurring of the lines between what is a blog and what is more traditional media. Traditional media owners have adopted blogs and blog like functions into their sites. (The BBC and *The Guardian* are at the vanguard.) Bloggers have become more professional, acting as journalists rather than the amateur enthusiasts they once were. This has far-reaching future implications for the PR industry as a whole.

NOTES

1   A. Hui, *Word-of-mouth the most powerful selling tool: Nielsen Global Survey*, Hong Kong: The Nielsen Company Online, 2007 Available HTTP: <http://asiapacific.acnielsen.com/news/20071002.shtml> (accessed 19 December 2008)
2   S. Elliott, *Letting Consumers Control Marketing: Priceless*: The New York Times, New York: The New York Times Company Online, 2006. Available HTTP: <http://www.nytimes.com/2006/10/09/business/media/09adcol.html> (accessed 20 December 2008)
3   Various *State of the Blogosphere*: Technorati: USA: Technorati, Inc Online, 2004–2009 Available HTTP: <http://technorati.com/state-of-the-blogosphere/> (accessed 5 January 2008)
4   Wikipedia contributors. Webmaster. Wikipedia, The Free Encyclopaedia Online, 2008. Available HTTP: <http://en.wikipedia.org/wiki/Blog> (accessed 5 January 2008)
5   C. Dellarocas, X. Zhang and N. Awad, 'Exploring the Value of Online Product Reviews in Forecasting Sales', *Journal of Interactive Marketing* Volume 21 / Number 4 / Autumn 2007 (p 23–45)
6   Various *State of the Blogosphere*: Technorati: USA: Technorati, Inc Online, 2004–2009. Available HTTP: <http://technorati.com/state-of-the-blogosphere/> (accessed 5 January 2008)
7   You can see the blogs here www.lgblog.co.uk, www.lglbog.de, www.lgblog.fr, www.lgblog.es and www.lgbog.it

5

Enacting corporate citizenship in Korea

Novartis Korea's five-generation families campaign

YUNNA RHEE, HYUNKI MOON
AND JEEYOON LEE

Novartis Korea is a part of the multinational pharmaceutical company Novartis Group, which is based in Switzerland. The Novartis Group operates in 140 countries, and Novartis Korea was established in 1997 through a merger. Novartis Korea in particular has been focusing its efforts in the pharmaceutical research and development area. Because of this strategic direction, Novartis Korea's commitment as a corporate citizen was not well known to the Korean market.

Novartis Korea hoped to let Koreans know that it was committed to playing an active role in promoting healthier and happier lives of Koreans. Fleishman-Hillard Korea was put in charge of designing a campaign that was tailored to the Korean cultural context and would enable Novartis Korea to enact its role as a responsible corporate citizen.

INTRODUCTION

Rapidly aging populations are a problem for societies around the world. Korea, however, is leading this worrisome trend with the fastest aging population of all and the lowest birth rate.

Calculations predict that Korea will become an 'age heavy' society by the year 2026 with 20 percent of the country's population consisting of individuals over the age of 65. With an exceptionally low birth rate and rapidly aging population, Korea faces realistic concerns over how to handle the ensuing issues which are already presenting themselves.

As traditional reverence for the elderly diminishes and appeal towards the nuclear family increases, prolonged retirements will become an increasingly heavy burden for both the nation and individual families to bear. The most significant burden in caring for the elderly would be providing quality health care. One of the core missions for Novartis is to provide quality health care products and services to both patients and non-patients. Novartis Korea saw an opportunity to showcase their commitment as a responsible corporate citizen in light of Korea's low birth rate and aging problem.

RESEARCH

Preliminary research for the campaign was conducted in order to understand the low birthrate and aging problem in Korea.

Literature on low birth rate and aging population was gathered from the Korea National Statistical Office (KNSO), the Samsung Economic Research Institute (SERI), the Ministry of Health, Welfare and Family Affairs (MHWFA) and the Korean Medical Association (KMA).

Through the preliminary research, 'family' was identified as the core entity that directly reflects a society's level of health and well-being. In Korea, there is a saying that reads ' 家和萬事成 [ga-wha-man-sa-sung],' which means that all goes well when one's home is harmonious. This Chinese expression indicates that you and your descendents would lead a good life if you respect elders, you be good to your parents and there is strong brotherhood and sisterhood in your family. Most Koreans learn this expression at school and they agree and sympathize with it.

It was also found that Korea currently is a society primarily consisting of three-generation families. This is a phenomenon that was in part caused by the low birth rate and deconstruction of the extended family system.

The 'Finding five-generation families (5GF) spanning one hundred years' campaign was a natural outgrowth of the research process. The 5GF campaign was based on the 家和萬事成 concept. It would address the issue of fast aging population coupled with the low birth rate through the stories of 5GFs. In order to 1) identify existing 5GFs, 2) find out more information about how Korean people thought of their families and lifestyles and 3) compare 5GFs' lifestyles to those of non-5GFs, the following research was conducted.

Two online surveys in conjunction with the launch of a campaign homepage site (www.5gfamily.co.kr) were implemented. These included a lifestyle survey on the general public and a separate lifestyle survey for those who identified themselves as 5GFs. A total of 6,928 people participated in the survey.

GOAL AND OBJECTIVES

The goal of the campaign was for Novartis Korea to be positioned as a socially responsible company that contributes to the well-being of Korean people. Specific objectives of the campaign were as follows:

- to raise public compassion and appreciation of the values and activities associated with a healthy and happy family life by celebrating 5GFs;

- to raise awareness of the importance of maintaining a healthy lifestyle through images of vibrant and thriving 5GFs.

COMMUNICATION STRATEGIES AND TACTICS

Strategies used were as follows:

- Demonstrate commitment to rekindling traditional family values – the foundation of a strong and healthy society – through moving and heartwarming 5GF stories. Use a variety of research methods to obtain personal anecdotes on the secrets of a happy and healthy 5GF for compelling campaign exposure and inspiration.
- Build widespread awareness and public interaction through strategic partnerships with the Ministry of Health, Welfare and Family Affairs and the Korean Medical Association thereby encouraging nationwide participation.
- In an effort to maximize participation, incorporate the integrated marketing communication (IMC) concept, utilizing various vehicles and tactics to arouse curiosity and interest surrounding the campaign. In addition, tailor the communication tools, such as online channels (e.g. campaign website) targeting the younger participants and offline channels (e.g. call centre) targeting the elderly participants, in order to appeal to and encourage participation from both the young and the elderly.
- Schedule campaign peak to take place in November. This peak month is strategically positioned between Korean Thanksgiving and the beginning of a new season, when families gather and celebrate the holidays.

Based on these strategies, the following tactics were employed:

- The symbol for the 5GF campaign was created for use in various communication efforts. The symbol was inspired by the image of a traditional Korean house. It conveys a happy 5GF and the writing '5代' seen on top of the logo reads '5 generations'. In Asian culture, the family is commonly compared to a tree. Images of trees were used as important visual metaphors during the campaign.
- The campaign was officially launched with ads in top-tier nationwide newspapers and the dissemination of press releases. In addition, an official motivation document encouraging cooperation, campaign posters and application forms were distributed to areas of the country with higher longevity rates and to health centres, hospitals and clinics across the country. To maintain steady interest during the two-month 5GF application period, newspaper advertising and press releases were evenly distributed, along with ongoing strategic media communications.
- The results of the on-line survey were distributed in press releases throughout the campaign as a means of maintaining media focus. They were later were used in a lifestyle comparison between the general public and 5GFs.
- Through additional phone and email surveys, the agency gathered information on 5GFs' lifestyle factors, such as demographics, health status, health tips and habits. From this information the agency drew meaningful insight, such as details on 5GF characteristics and factors associated with a healthy, big family.

Figure 5.1 Logo and newspaper advert ("We're searching for 5-generation families in Korea")

Figure 5.2 Campaign website ("The 5-generation family search")

- A gala-styled 5GF event was organized. Participating families from across the country gathered to celebrate their happiness, health and strong family ties.
  - The event included an introduction to the campaign's result, congratulatory remarks from community leaders, an awards ceremony and entertainment.
  - Six out of 26 5GFs were chosen for their outstanding stories, including the one with the most offspring and another for incredible tales of bonding. These families received special recognition.
  - Prior to the highly-styled gathering, the agency organized a press conference to introduce the results of the 5GF campaign and lifestyle survey.
  - In preparation for strategic media pitching, the agency pre-interviewed the 5GFs to collect compelling and touching stories. The agency collaborated with top-tier media, including TV and national daily newspapers, in advance. As a result, a wide variety of angles not previously introduced received extensive coverage.
  - A surprise first birthday party for one family's great-great-grandson was organized. This resulted in the image of his 100-year-old great-great-grandmother helping him to cut his traditional celebratory rice cake. This garnered extensive media coverage.
  - The immensely popular 'great-great-grandmother arm wrestling' activity met with cheers and laughter by all those in attendance. The incredibly entertaining and special atmosphere was captured in dynamic detail and resulted in numerous photo reports.

Figure 5.3 Five generations

Figure 5.4 Birthday cake

Figure 5.5 Arm wrestle

EXECUTION TIMELINE

The campaign strategies and tactics were implemented in the following order. First, Fleishman-Hillard Korea and Novartis Korea constructed an advisory committee for the 5GF campaign. It was comprised of medical doctors, government officials from the Ministry of Health, Welfare and Family Affairs, managers from Novartis Korea, health care researchers and humanities scholars. Second, the online survey was conducted in conjunction with the campaign website launch. At this point, applications for the 5GF event were accepted. Third, the second set of lifestyle surveys on 5GFs was conducted. Six 5GFs who had special family stories were selected through an open essay competition. Fourth, press conferences were arranged to promote the upcoming 5GF event. Fifth, the gala-styled 5GF event was held at one of the major hotels in Seoul, Korea.

TARGET AUDIENCE

As the campaign opted to raise national awareness and appreciation of healthy familial life, Korean people were set to be the target audience.

Results/Evaluation

* The campaign identified 26 5GFs.
* The campaign drew nationwide interest and resulted in exceptionally favourable media coverage. 306 articles were published on the 5GF campaign. The campaign

Figure 5.6 In the media

was covered on TV 23 times. Media impressions totalled 124,944,400. Online banner impressions totalled 31,577,324.

- The campaign received favourable feedback from the media directly connected to positive impressions of Novartis Korea. The annual media audit assessing the preferences of health care journalists showed an increased preference towards Novartis Korea (compared to the 2006 results).
- Participants in the campaign expressed positive attitudes: Pal-Boon Ahn, one of the oldest grandmother participants, said, 'Today is the happiest day of my whole life.' Another participant, Eun-Wha Park, said, 'We had a great time during this campaign. It was very memorable.'
- Awards won include the 2007 Asia-Pacific PR Awards Corporate Social Responsibility Campaign of the Year and the 2007 Korea PR Awards Corporate Image PR.

UPDATE

- The 5GF campaign created social momentum that served to remind the public of the value of health and family. Although the campaign ended, as of 2008, the agency is still receiving inquiries from broadcast outlets interested in covering the 5GF stories.
- Reflecting the continuous attention to and interest in the 5GF campaign, Novartis Korea and Korean Medical Association (KMA) published a book entitled *The 5GF Stories* this year. It celebrates the campaign's second anniversary and KMA's centennial anniversary.

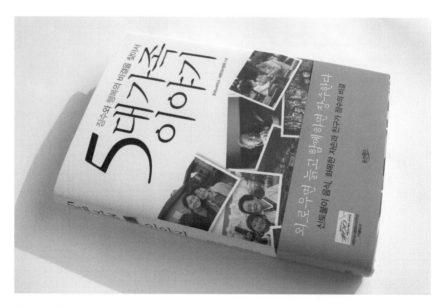

Figure 5.7 Storybook

LESSONS LEARNED

- Understanding the local culture is essential for designing an effective public relations campaign. The campaign is a good example of a global pharmaceutical company, along with its public relations agency, executing a creative corporate social responsibility campaign based on the deep understanding of, interest in and respect for the local people and their culture.
- The campaign showed that research can be also used as a way to increase awareness and interest about the campaign. More specifically, the survey results can be utilized as additional news sources. Participation in a survey can generate more interest about a campaign.
- A strong theme is timeless. Regardless of time, the public pays attention to and shows interest in classic topics like family and health.
- Heartwarming storytelling is a powerful way to increase PR impact.
- One drawback of the 5GF campaign is the limited exposure and presence of Novartis Korea. This, however, was anticipated, especially on television news programs and in newspaper articles, because of the campaign's public nature. What is more important is the fact that the campaign received favourable feedback from the media. This feedback was directly connected to positive impressions of Novartis among healthcare journalists, professionals and healthcare communities.

6

Taking the time to listen, learn and act

An example of complex international dialogue

PETER OSBORNE AND ROBBIE HUSTON

INTRODUCTION

It is important to place the subject of this work into an historical context. BNFL, a nuclear services company, had serious public and political acceptability issues in the early 1980s. Concerns stemmed from attitudes developed during the Cold War years when the nuclear industry was fabled for being shrouded in secrecy. As a result, the public and the media found it difficult to separate their understanding of the civil nuclear industry from its historical military associations. To compound matters a series of nuclear incidents at Sellafield – the fire of 1957 and the beach incident of 1983 – produced a very negative image of the industry. Public concern and focus were magnified by a sensitized media.

The beach incident, in which radioactivity from the Sellafield site was found on the coastline near the Sellafield site, was closely followed by a Yorkshire TV documentary. The documentary, *Sellafield – the nuclear laundry*, claimed to expose an alleged cluster of leukaemia linked to the site. Despite the fact that no causal link between Sellafield and leukaemia clusters had ever been established, this coverage blighted Sellafield's reputation for years.

For PR practitioners in the industry, this was particularly challenging. Initial research concluded that people's overriding perception of Sellafield was that it was dishonest and secretive. In response, a PR strategy that sought to demystify Sellafield and its activities was developed. Emerging from this, the company's open door policy invited the public to go to Sellafield and judge for themselves. In addition, nine million newspaper advertisements were printed and, in support, the media were invited to travel to Sellafield aboard the Flying Scotsman from cities across the UK. A new visitors centre was built and for the first time the public could tour the site. In its first year alone, a massive 175,000 visitors came. As a result, there were significant gains in the favourability rating of the site in before and after opinion polls conducted by MORI.

This approach was described by BNFL senior PR management as the 'starting and continuation of dialogue'. Crucial to the success of the campaign was the drive of a new chairman, Sir Christopher Harding. Sir Christopher fully supported this approach. Recruited from outside the nuclear industry in 1986, he was instrumental in rolling back the veil of secrecy. Consequently, the negative perceptions of Sellafield continued to decrease. However, as the world entered a new technological age the green movement burgeoned, it soon became apparent that organizations faced with making environmental decisions would encounter fresh challenges. BNFL, despite its improved image, would be no different.

STAKEHOLDER DIALOGUE

1995 was a watershed year for corporate environmental decision making in the UK. The traditional model of decide, announce and defend (DAD) had been used by Shell UK. The DAD model was tested to the full during its efforts of their oil storage platform *Brent Spar*. Having gained the support of the UK government but under the onslaught of a successful political and public campaign and direct action from Greenpeace, Shell UK reversed their initial decision and chose to decommission the *Brent Spar* on land.

Mindful of a sea change of greater stakeholder inclusion that followed Shell's reversal and easier access to information, BNFL, faced with issues of its own, undertook a review of its environmental decision-making process. In the 1990s it had been locked into confrontational relationships with a variety of pressure groups and non-governmental organizations upon which the open door policy had had little, if any impact. Engaging The Environment Council, an organization well respected for its work in mediating environmental disputes, BNFL embarked upon an ambitious dialogue that invited any stakeholders with an interest in their activities to participate. Its aim was 'to inform their decision-making process about the improvement of their environmental performance in the context of their overall development'. Through it BNFL sought to gain a greater understanding of stakeholder's interests and concerns.

The long and extremely thorough process involving local, national and international stakeholders that took place between 1998 and 2004 changed BNFL's attitude and approach towards stakeholder consultation. Considering an alternative model of define, agree and implement (DAI), while reserving the right to make its own decisions, they embraced vital elements of dialogue introduced by The Environment Council. These elements, including jointly agreed agendas and reports, were later put to good use in the dialogue with Norwegian stakeholders (see below).

Figure 6.1 Aerial view of Sellafield plant

STAKEHOLDER ENGAGEMENT

In the new millennium the Sellafield site attracted the interests of Norwegian stake-holders. By 2003 the Bellona Foundation had visited the Sellafield site three times, the Norwegian Ambassador to London had visited once and the Landsorganisasjonen I Norge (LO), the Norwegian equivalent of the Trades Union Council, had also visited once. Each party was able to come away from Sellafield with a much better understanding of the site's activities and environmental impacts. A Joint Sellafield Conference held in 2003 was an attempt to bring together all relevant UK and Norwegian stakeholders to enable a much better understanding of each others' interests and concerns. Politicians, government officials, representatives from local communities, regulators, trade unionists and local businesses came together to listen, learn and debate.

The most progressive output from the BNFL National Stakeholder Dialogue were reports produced jointly by the participants. Arguably more important was the fundamental impact on BNFL's culture which occurred through engaging in the process with stakeholders during the six years of dialogue. The company embraced The Environment Council's beliefs that better mutual understanding leads to better decisions, stakeholders have a right to be heard and, importantly, change is possible.

Its representatives witnessed the benefits of a more inclusive approach to environmental decision making through the following principles:

- Identify all stakeholders affected by the decision.
- Understand their interests and concerns.

- Jointly agree process and agenda.
- Mutually develop trust with stakeholders.
- Share information, even that of a confidential and sensitive nature.

BNFL's early relationship with the Norwegian stakeholders had consisted of two strands. The first was of suspicion and fear – suspicion of what action they might be plotting and individuals that engagement could be detrimental to their careers. The safety of non-commitment and minimal engagement was more often than not the preferred choice. Second, there was a prevailing attitude of having a legitimate right to carry out operations without interference from outsiders. Put simply, why should the company engage with people whose ultimate goal was to close down operations? A major challenge for the BNFL practitioners was to break down these attitudes. An important element of the process was learning about and understanding the interests and concerns of the stakeholders in both the UK and Norway.

RESEARCH

At an early stage the BNFL communication team recognized that it needed a better understanding of the stakeholders involved. They undertook a comprehensive review of the stakeholders, their concerns, interests and motivations and the dynamics that existed between them. As a consequence of this, Norwegian stakeholders were invited to meetings and site visits as part of a joint fact-finding mission.

Through meeting and discussing with key Norwegians, such as Bellona and the Norwegian Government (through the London Embassy), the BNFL communications team was able to gain a clearer understanding of who the key Norwegian stakeholders were. By hosting a UK seminar that included several key players, such as the Department for Trad and Industry (DTI), the Foreign and Commonwealth Office (FCO) and the Department for Food and Rural Affairs (Defra), BNFL was able to more fully identify the UK stakeholders and their interests.

As the dialogue progressed and a potential technological solution emerged, it became clear that if there was to be any further progress, additional stakeholders such as the regulators and the nuclear waste executive, UK Nirex, would have to become fully engaged.

Sensing that a solution may be possible, Norwegian Environment Minister Borge Brende escalated the issue. Writing to then Secretary of State Margaret Beckett, Brende implored the UK to introduce a moratorium on discharges and investigate the use of the chemical tetraphenylphosphonium bromide (TPP) and the discharges containing the radioactive isotope Tc99.

The UK's willingness to permit a trial use of TPP was dependent on the approval from Nirex that not only would the use of TPP work effectively but the resulting waste could be treated, packaged and stored safely on land. Nirex was concerned that there were uncertainties about the long-term, safe and sustainable storage of waste containing radioactive waste and TPP.

OBJECTIVES

BNFL's objectives changed as the dialogue developed and trust developed between the players. The primary objective was to protect the company's reputation. One tactic was to contain the issue to Norwegian stakeholders. The rationale was that the more exposure the issue received, the greater the risk of others being drawn in, thereby compounding the issue and making it more difficult to manage.

An underlying objective was to ensure that the Norwegians were provided with relevant information in an understandable manner. As the two governments got drawn into the process, BNFL's objective broadened to attempt to protect the UK government from exposure and, when required, to give full support. The UK government had enjoyed an excellent bi-lateral and long-standing relationship with Norway. The only two issues with which there was disharmony were whaling and Sellafield. They had contained the Sellafield issue until the late 1990s. As more environmental evidence became available to suggest that discharges from the site were reaching the coast of Norway, and more Norwegian stakeholders became involved, management of the issue became in danger of running out of control.

As the issue developed into an international affair, the BNFL team worked towards locking the UK and Norwegian communities together in dialogue. Trade unionist met with trade unionist, fisherman with fisherman, councillor with councillor and so on. This produced a greater knowledge of each others' needs and concerns, engendering greater trust and some personal bonding between individuals.

COMMUNICATIONS STRATEGY

The aim of the communications strategy was to engage with key stakeholders in what was clearly a sensitive and controversial issue. Although it was accepted by critical stakeholders that there was no evidence that the discharge of the radioactive isotope Tc99 into the Irish Sea presented any health or environmental impact, there was a perception of Nordic stakeholders that, as these discharges were increasing, their concerns could at some future point become a reality. There was also a growing stakeholder concern, led by Lofoten mot Sellafield and Bellona, that the discharges could have an economic impact on their international market for seafood, especially cod, caught in Norwegian waters.

The BNFL view was that engaging with Nordic stakeholders, primarily Bellona and Lofoten mot Sellafield, was preferable to a confrontational approach. The tactics used were:

- Be open and honest with stakeholders.
- Talk and meet regularly.
- Share information.
- Develop close personal relationships.
- Jointly record and agree actions to avoid potential misunderstandings.

TARGET AUDIENCES

Stakeholders fell largely into the Sellafield community, UK government and regulators and Nordic stakeholders. The Sellafield community included the Sellafield Local Liaison Committee, which represented a cross-section of the local community and trades unions. Due to the UK government ownership of BNFL, a number of government departments and organizations had an interest in its operations, including the then DTI, Defra, FCO, the Environment Agency and Nirex, as well as UK embassies in Norway and Iceland. Nordic stakeholders included the community group LmS and NGO Bellona, the Norwegian government, especially their environment department, Norwegian regulators, academics, the Norwegian and Icelandic embassies and the Nordic Council.

CAMPAIGN

The turning point in the relationship with Bellona and Lofoten mot Sellafield was the agreement to hold a joint international conference on solutions for the discharge of Tc99 near Sellafield. The conference culminated with a joint closing statement, part of which read:

> The Conference has enabled all participants to achieve a better understanding of each other's respective positions. The organising bodies are pleased with the progress made to date and remain committed to the process of constructive dialogue that has culminated in the conference.

Until this time, the relationship had been predominantly confrontational. A conference, to which BNFL was not invited, had already been held in Norway, but Nordic stakeholders were keen to hold a conference in Sellafield's backyard. This was initially met with extreme caution by both senior BNFL managers and the community around Sellafield, which felt that this would be a direct threat to local jobs. Lofoten mot Sellafield's stated aim at this stage was that Sellafield should be closed down. Consequently, a lot of work was put in by the BNFL communications team to persuade UK stakeholders that the conference should go ahead. This included meetings with senior BNFL managers to discuss the proposal and an assessment of the risks and opportunities using a strengths, weaknesses, opportunities and threats (SWOT) analysis. The Foreign and Commonwealth Office welcomed the idea of a conference and was keen to be involved. Other government departments were initially less keen.

Extensive preparation took place in the six months leading up to the conference in April 2003. Exploratory discussions took place between the BNFL communications team, Bellona and Lofoten mot Sellafield in Oslo to agree a way forward, including a Memorandum of Understanding to build trust. Agreement was reached in principle to co-host an international conference with Bellona and Lofoten mot Sellafield. A key principle of the conference was that it should be based on scientific – as opposed to anecdotal – information. The conference itinerary was to include a visit to the site for the Norwegian stakeholders so they could learn about plants and activities.

Weekly teleconferences took place between Norway and the BNFL communications team in the UK. During the teleconferences, the agenda, content, format, speakers and an agreement on who should chair the conference were discussed. The resulting actions were recorded and agreed by all parties. There was a period of highly intense and sensitive negotiation over the content and format of the conference, including who should present and in what order they should speak. Agreement on the chairing of the conference was a particularly contentious issue and the legitimacy of the chairperson was crucial to the conference. It was recognized by all parties that participants would have to have confidence in the impartiality of the selected person. It was agreed that there should be a joint chairing; a Norwegian bishop and a UK environmental expert were identified to each chair one day of the two-day conference.

A balance was sought between UK and Nordic stakeholders and it was recognized that the community around Sellafield needed extensive representation. At the same time, there was acknowledgement that the views of Nordic stakeholders held legitimacy. The final conference line-up included Bellona, Lofoten mot Sellafield, BNFL's Environment and Health and Safety Director, the UK Environment Agency, representatives from West Cumbrian and Norwegian local councils, Chairman of the Sellafield Local Liaison Committee, UK and Norwegian trade unions and local businesses. The keynote speaker was the then Norwegian Environment Minister, Børge Brende.

It was also agreed that the best way to understand a complex technical issue was to invite the conference participants to visit the Sellafield site, including the enhanced actinide removal plant (EARP), the waste treatment plant from which Tc99 was discharged.

The conference had several positive outcomes; not least of these outcomes was that a better understanding was gained by all participants. A possible technological solution was identified and discussed. Technical evidence produced by the UK and Norwegian regulators helped to reassure the Norwegian stakeholders that existing levels of Tc99 did not pose a risk to the health of Norwegian people. All of these were captured in a joint concluding statement.

Box 6.1 Sellafield Conference to Discuss the Effects of Tc99: Concluding Statement

---

The conference to discuss the effects of technetium-99 (Tc99) involving BNFL, the Bellona Foundation and Lofoten mot Sellafield took place at Summergrove Hall, near Sellafield on 22nd and 23rd April 2003.

The conference was addressed by a wide variety of speakers, considering the health, environmental, economic, social and political implications of these discharges in the Nordic countries and the UK.

The conference has enabled all participants to achieve a better understanding of each other's respective positions. The organising bodies are pleased with the progress made to date and remain committed to the process of constructive dialogue that has culminated in the conference.

Technetium–99 discharges have been routinely monitored in the North Atlantic.

The organising bodies recognise that perceptions of Tc99 in Norway could present an economic risk to the Norwegian marine harvest industry. However, the organising bodies also recognise that Tc99 currently does not pose a health risk to the Norwegian population.

Lofoten mot Sellafield and the Bellona Foundation recognize that BNFL has applied to the UK regulatory authorities for permission to undertake a plant trial of the TPP process. Lofoten mot Sellafield and Bellona now respectfully request that the UK authorities grant permission for this trial to take place.

Lofoten mot Sellafield and Bellona wish to see an immediate cessation of the Tc99 discharges from Sellafield and believe it is possible to implement an immediate twelve month cessation of Tc99 discharges from Sellafield to allow further investigation of potential abatement technologies. Whilst respecting this position BNFL believes that such action raises significant issues and at this point in time is not practical.

In conclusion the organising bodies also recognised the primacy of national and international policy in the area of radioactive waste management and discharges, and remain committed to seeking further progress within that context.

Nordic politicians, officials, including the Icelandic Environment Minister, and the media were encouraged to visit Sellafield while senior BNFL experts invested considerable time to discuss the issues with key stakeholders. There was close cooperation with the UK embassies in Oslo and Reykjavik and the Norwegian embassy in London. This involved several face-to-face meetings with the embassies in Norway and Iceland, as well as return visits to Sellafield to see for themselves, describe the complex nuclear processes and help to improve their understanding of the issues. They could in turn provide context when engaging with the media and other interested parties in their respective countries.

RESULTS/EVALUATION

Further discussions at the bilateral level resulted in UK Secretary of State Margaret Beckett authorizing the trial use of TPP to separate Tc99 from medium active concentrate (MAC), a liquid by-product from reprocessing Magnox spent fuel. After successful trials and further research by Nirex, TPP was introduced into the waste treatment process that enabled discharges of Tc99 from Sellafield to be reduced by 90 per cent.

The success of the technological solution resulted in significant developments within the stakeholder community. The Lofoten islanders disbanded Lofoten mot Sellafield. They announced their decision at a celebration entitled 'Together we did it', which was held in the Lofoten Islands in June 2004. In commemoration, a plaque was unveiled by the Norwegian Environment Minister in Stamsund in the Lofoten Islands. Many key stakeholders, including representatives from the Norwegian and UK governments and BNFL, attended.

A wealth of plaudits was received from Nordic and UK ministers, regulators, local communities, the media and Bellona:

> The close contact between Norwegian and British politicians, expert authorities and the industry has been a highly positive experience . . . I have come to firmly believe in this kind of co-operation in order to solve complicated international problems.
>
> Børge Brende, Norwegian Environment Minister

> The Tc99 discharge has now been stopped. BNFL can take a great deal of credit for a resolution that was achieved without any losers.
>
> The Nordic Council

Figure 6.2 Norwegian Environment Minister Børge Brende (left) with BNFL's Head of Health and Safety John Clarke (right) at Sellafield

This cooperation with BNFL started with a certain amount of scepticism, went soon to dialogue and ended with happiness. This dialogue and co-operation gave us the result that we dreamt about.

Lofton mot Sellafield

Media evaluation revealed extensive positive Nordic coverage.

A mature dialogue, based on trust and respect, is now firmly established between British Nuclear Group and Norway. It has been described by the Norwegians as a 'model'.

In 2005, the campaign won the CIPR Gold Award in the Stakeholder Relationship Management Programme Engagement category which looked for outstanding examples of how stakeholder management could be used to address complicated issues.

In awarding gold, the judges said that the British Nuclear Group entry demonstrated clear objectives and a very structured approach to a highly sensitive issue and that it was a complex campaign that required a high level of planning and research. They added that the team had managed to work a number of complex relationships, including government ministers, and showed that good relationships need to be nurtured and developed.

LESSONS LEARNED

- Dialogue needs to be maintained to be effective in the long term. Dialogue after the introduction of TPP became less frequent. A contained leak of radioactive liquid within a reprocessing plant (Thorp) at Sellafield in 2004 was perceived by Norway to have been slowly communicated to the Norwegian government and stakeholders. Information was gathered from the media and opposition groups resulting in a skewed perception of the event. As a consequence, the Norwegians expressed their dissatisfaction and despite the fact that there was no release of radioactivity to the environment, commenced a new 'Shut Thorp' campaign. This remains the policy of the Norwegian government. Trust has had to be rebuilt.
- The case illustrates the benefit of having a small close-knit team which in this case was managed by BNFL communications working with and bringing in other parts of the business, such as Health and Safety, Operations and Research and Development. The communications team, comprised of two public affairs specialists and a media specialist, were able to identify stakeholders, who impacted or could impact on the issue. This helped them to understand the issues, identify what was possible and then make it happen.
- The communications team played an important role in keeping the engagement on track, while maintaining trust in the process. For example, when necessary, they provided reassurance to senior managers when their support for the engagement process appeared to be wavering. The communications team proactively listened to their concerns and was able to remind them of the bigger picture so that minor setbacks would not derail the overall process. In larger organizations, securing and keeping senior management support is crucial.

- It is important to get the facts to stakeholders so that they can make informed decisions and allay any fears or misconceptions.
- The case illustrates the increasing importance of 24/7 media operations, the importance of the internet to take the initiative away from organizations and how important it is to monitor and correct misleading reporting. As a consequence of the dialogue, information, including press releases, appeared on a number of international websites. It was important for the communications team to be fully aware of this coverage and to correct it as necessary.
- The success of this dialogue became the template for future international engagement by the company.

7

Setting up an effective press office for a professional body

GERALD CHAN

Our understanding of modern public relations practice is that it is a discipline situated firmly within senior management and used as a strategic communication tool that protects and enhances an organization's reputation.

The general definition of public relations, as adopted by the UK Chartered Institute of Public Relations (CIPR), is that it is 'what you say, what you do and what others may have to say about you'. As a concept, this is applicable across different organizations and at all levels within an organization. However, therein ends the application of the idea. There are other subtleties involved in media relations and the aim to engage in public relations activities for a press officer is far more complex than is commonly assumed.

This case examines the experience of setting up and running a successful press office for a professional body. It does not seek to provide an academic analysis of how different public relations theories can be adapted and explained within the context of a press office, but it does provide a case study with practical knowledge on building and maintaining a viable press office function within an organization.

BACKGROUND

The Royal College of Obstetricians and Gynaecologists (RCOG) is a professional body for those working as hospital consultants in women's healthcare. Its slogan is 'Setting standards to improve women's health'. It achieves its slogan's aim through the publication of Working Party reports and clinical standards and guidelines. It is involved in the advancement of the specialty of obstetrics and gynaecology (O&G) through encouraging medical research into women's reproductive medicine and health care. It also designs and delivers postgraduate medical education and training programmes. Alongside these activities, the RCOG makes submissions to national and international consultations in medicine and its members contribute to government and National Health Service (NHS) policy.

The RCOG's remit and the consequences of its work are therefore as wide as they are far-reaching. There are many daily issues with which the RCOG press office deals on behalf of the discipline. The common ones are: gynaecological cancers, maternal and perinatal death, antenatal screening, premature birth, fertility treatment and contraceptive care. The press office is very busy, but its work was limited as it was confined to reactive PR and it did not have a public affairs role to complement its communications work.

It was decided in 2005 that there was a need to expand the RCOG's PR department of one press officer to include a public affairs officer, a marketing officer, a departmental secretary and a head of communications. The head of communications (this author) was appointed in 2006. The rest of this case examines the thinking and decisions that went into developing an efficient press office that deals both reactively and proactively, while engaging with a wider group of stakeholders other than the media.

THE BEGINNING

The new head of communications had a huge task ahead as it was virtually a fresh start. Although the role was new to the organization and there were many opportunities to develop the communications function, it was clear that because of this period of change, there was an expectation that certain non-traditional public relations roles were included in the communications remit. There was the issue of the way in which the press office functioned previously and whether improvements or changes could be made in order to make it work better. It was important to ensure that any adjustments to the way work was carried out included proof that adjustments would deliver results and were not a matter of change for change's sake, as is often the case following a regime change.

It was clear at the beginning that there was one key area requiring immediate attention. In order to understand the working environment and the expectations of the PR function within the organization, research into the organization's culture, including its structures and hierarchies, and the roles and workings of each directorate was needed. It was noted that some departments may undertake varying degrees of marketing communications work, such as corporate branding or stakeholder communications, and it was crucial to analyze who had responsibility for these activities and how these activities were carried out. An understanding of these elements would help in producing a mapping document from which public relations communications could be discerned (i.e. the PR needs of the organization), situated (i.e. where PR fits in each) and implemented (i.e. the deliverables according to resources).

CONTEXTUAL AND BENCHMARKING RESEARCH

In the first weeks, meetings were set up with heads of departments and directors to understand the role of each directorate. Information such as managerial responsibilities and reporting structures were noted, as were the expectations that each had on the role of PR and communications within the organization. A range of resources was also researched. These included corporate information on the website, annual reports, historical information about the evolution of the department from committee minutes and documents dealing with organizational strategy. From this initial investigation, a draft outline of the role of public relations and communications within the organization was developed. This was contrasted to the textbook knowledge of PR. Principles such as Grunig's situational theory and the four models of PR and roles theory were used to understand the extent of the PR function within the organization.

The first impression of the work of the press office, as practised then, was that it was a public information provider through a two-way asymmetrical flow of communications.

The next step was to conduct a comparative review of how PR is practised in similar organizations. There exists an informal network of press officers and PR managers working in the other royal medical colleges and in healthcare PR. A brief survey was devised to understand the role of PR in these organizations and then distributed to all contacts. Information such as the size of the PR department, type of PR practised and the common PR techniques employed was collated. This survey provided useful information on how other similar organizations conducted and evaluated their PR activities, whether there was any crossover with other communications functions and whether there was anything to be learned about PR tactics from these professionals. Benchmarking metrics, such as the use of key performance indicators and the setting of targets, were noted, as was best practice in the running of a busy press office.

At this stage, it was clear that there was much scope for in-house PR in health care organizations but it was mostly confined to a technical role although there were aspirations to enhance the PR offering so that it included some elements of strategic communications, public affairs and campaigning. In organizations where there was the close interplay between policy and advocacy with public relations, these organizations tended to be more strategic in their outlook. It must also be noted that in these organizations, the PR function was more firmly embedded and their departmental budgets were larger.

Finally, there was mutual recognition among all surveyed that the potential of PR would be realized when it had access to the dominant coalition. However, because of the hierarchical nature of most health care organizations, influence is often sought and obtained through a slow process of drip-feeding ideas to those with power and legitimacy before change can commence. In some cases, third-party endorsement was used so that the PR role was appreciated and respected.

OBJECTIVE SETTING

Based on the research and the assessment of the communications needs and capabilities of the College, two sets of objectives were set. The first set of objectives focused on the overall objectives for undertaking communications and these referenced the organizational strategy. An example is: 'To raise awareness about the College as the custodian of standards in women's healthcare'. The second set of objectives had to be measurable and outcome-oriented, seeking to ensure that communications activities were planned and complemented individual strands of the College's work. An example is: 'To develop a process to respond to media calls about a medical condition and/or treatments, supported by robust, peer-reviewed scientific evidence'.

After examining the immediate objectives and how they were to be achieved, individual strategies were developed for the press office and the public relations and public affairs functions. These documents took the form of a traditional strategy document with an analysis of the environment and the challenges confronting the organization. After identifying the issues and stakeholders involved, they had to set out the intention to communicate and proposed solutions in the form of key messages and tactics. These strategies are then used as a reference template for future promotional work. In other words, should there be a future campaign on an issue, the objectives, press lines and positioning would be drawn from these strategic documents, and tailored to the campaign as appropriate.

DECIDING ON TARGET AUDIENCES

It is important to remember who your main stakeholders are when setting your objectives. As the College works in an issues-laden area and is involved in a range of medically-oriented activities which impact on health care service provision, a basic stakeholder mapping exercise was undertaken to understand the groups of publics who have a direct or indirect impact on the organization based on their claims to legitimacy, power and urgency.

At the heart of the College's work is its relationship with the people it serves, that is, women of all ages, from the moment reproductive function starts until after menopause. Secondary to this core audience is the specialty itself, the College's membership, its governing body, the Council, junior doctors and other medical agencies and organizations. Other important stakeholder groups such as government, Parliament and the media follow.

As the purpose was to specifically examine the fundamental requirements needed to set up a press office, some of these stakeholder groups can be grouped together. The reason for this is that the press office is usually the first point of contact for all public queries, which includes patients seeking information and incoming national and international media queries from newspapers and broadcasters.

GETTING DOWN TO THE WORK

The success of any press office is measured not only by the number of press releases it issues or the number of press calls it receives per month (though it is safe to say that once relationships and trust are built with the media, the number of approaches should increase), but through its ability to provide response in a timely and relevant manner. For this to happen, it is important to have in place processes and procedures to ensure that news is filtered and managed accordingly. The processes are there to ensure that the strategic objectives and communications targets are met. They adapt to changes in technology and to the changes occurring within the organization.

TO COMMUNICATE, OR NOT TO COMMUNICATE

By the very nature of its work, a press office is reactive. A press call can come at any time of the day and during weekends. Sometimes the query requires research and further discussion; on other occasions a swift reply is all that is needed. Press office work is busy. At peak times, when dealing with newly released stories, it may feel like a production line where story after story is being dealt with.

In order to deal effectively with all media calls, it is important to have in place a system to monitor stories as they evolve in the news media. This can be done by scanning the newspapers and online news channels throughout the day. There are several methods to keep the press officer informed, such as real time news alerts from media monitoring companies, updates from newswires and press clipping agencies and RSS news feeds from online news outlets. There are also specialist sources of information, such as news on developments in Parliament or press releases issued by different government departments. Given that journalists sometimes get their stories from parliamentary questions, motions or debates, it is important to have a good political monitoring system set up so that press officers are aware of what is being said. As in the case of news monitoring, there are commercial organizations that provide political update services or you may conduct your own monitoring through Hansard and civil service web portals.

The advent of the citizen journalist and the importance placed on corporate social responsibility means that blogs, file- and video-sharing websites and social messaging and networking websites need to be monitored regularly. Pressure group and grassroots lobbying activities have stemmed from such conduits and it is important to know what some of these organizations or individuals are saying about your organization.

Effective monitoring of the news and social environments helps prepare a press officer to take media calls. The intelligence-gathering activity forms an integral part of the boundary-spanning role of public relations and ensures that the organization communicates effectively and in a timely manner. The next step in the building of process is the way in which a press officer would respond to queries.

Apart from deciding which communications tools to use (e.g. press release, holding statement, media briefing or press conference), the structure of the organization determines how quickly a response can be issued. It takes longer for copy approval to be granted in a bureaucratic organisation with a rigid chain of command or if the subject matter is technical or complex. These challenges need to be borne in mind when setting communications targets and careful planning by press officers is needed so that sign-off is obtained in good time.

The press officer speaking on behalf of the organization must be knowledgeable in the subject area if credibility is to be established with the media. On the occasions when comment cannot be provided because information required is of a specialist or esoteric nature, it is important to have to hand a list of trained media spokespeople who can handle these calls. Once briefed on the issues and news angles, their knowledge should take over; they are the experts and will be able to put across the organization's views with authority.

By prioritizing the issues and having a system to respond quickly and decisively to media queries, the press office will have fulfilled one of its aims, which is to be the first contact point for all media queries relating to the subject area.

MEASURING THE RESULTS OF PR

While gaining media coverage is important as it is the physical evidence of PR success, it is important to note if, within the publicity achieved, the organization's key messages have been picked up by the media. This could take the form of a mention of the organization, an aspect of a campaign in the newspapers or a sound bite on broadcast news. This is the most basic confirmation that communications have filtered through and it is essential for the press office to keep a record of these media mentions. Besides giving a picture of what journalists are saying and how the organization is being portrayed, such information could be used to inform future communications activity.

Traditionally, other measurements, such as the amount of column inches obtained or Advertising Value Equivalents (AVEs), were used to indicate and, in some cases, justify PR spend. There are more sophisticated methods to evaluate the success of communications, such as whether there has been a discernible attitudinal or behavioural change in target stakeholders. For example, in the case of a public health campaign to raise awareness about the harmful effects of maternal obesity, coverage obtained could be analyzed to see if the key messages appear in the media. In the longer term, more robust social scientific research could be undertaken to see if an increase in public awareness has led to changes in lifestyle among key groups within the population. However, the ability to develop these measurements and the levels of accuracy is mostly down to the resources available to the press officer.

The College press office produces a digest once every two months. It is distributed to Council members as proof of the amount of work carried out over the preceding months. It includes useful data such as the number of calls answered and media mentions received each month. It includes the number of press releases and statements issued and the subsequent coverage achieved via the different media channels. It provides a précis of parliamentary and political work undertaken and the results of such work. This document provides useful information on daily operational work and the issues encountered. It provides press officers with a tool from which to learn as trends and patterns in the media can be spotted over a period of time. The collated information is then fed back into future planning.

RESULTS AND EVALUATION

Having set up the press office, developed the necessary processes and implemented the strategy, it was important to ensure that the press office was able to account for its work. In the first year of the new press office (staffed by two press officers, including the head of department), output visibly increased by threefold. This was measured by the amount of communications activities undertaken and the amount of coverage subsequently received. Communications activities were quantified as the number of press calls received in a month, those calls that led to mentions in the media, the numbers of press releases and statements issued each month, and direct quotes arising from these activities. As the departmental budget was modest, it was difficult to conduct a more detailed study into media coverage other than the development of a basic mechanism to track whether stories in the media were negative/positive or neutral in reference to the College, where these stories appeared and which journalists were writing these stories.

Relationships with the main health and medical journalists from print, broadcast and online media were strengthened through regular contact. The College was frequently approached when comment on maternal and reproductive health was required. Informal targets on the time taken to handle press calls were often met. It was decided that targets would remain informal as the length of time taken to respond to calls would depend on the type of query, the amount of research and information required and the time taken to develop press lines and an official response.

Public affairs activities are an integral function within the communications mix and these were included in the evaluation. Performance was measured by the number of policy consultation submissions made, the numbers of parliamentary briefings held and the consequences of these activities, such as parliamentary questions asked and motions debated. While the College had previously focused on government relations in the policy work that it was engaged in, there was now greater awareness amongst MPs of the College's activities and its role in society. This was reflected in the good relationships formed with selected MPs and the way in which the College was approached when medical expertise within the specialty was sought.

CHANGING THE WAY WE WORK

The ultimate goal for any press office is to ensure that it learns from the mistakes it makes in order to improve its relationships with the media and be more responsive. With the advent of 24/7 media and the fast-paced nature of online news, some traditional methods of media relations are being replaced by new media techniques such as video-streaming and webcasting. Press offices need to adapt to these technological changes.

There is an unwritten etiquette in media relations and practice differs depending on the sector and field. These codes need to be noted by the press office if media relations are to be effective. A better understanding of the subtleties is gained through constant interaction with journalists, networking with communications peers and intelligence gathering.

The visible improvements in the work of the College press office after the first year, and the way in which the College's communications were beginning to make a difference in agenda-setting justified changing previous practice so that things could be done better and more efficiently. Staffing was rearranged within the team, bearing in mind also the talents and experience of incumbent press officers, so that the press office plays to its strengths and abilities. Other non-essential communications activities were prioritized. It is also important to note that the officers of the College, including the president, vice presidents, honorary treasurer, honorary secretary and chief executive, were aware of the positive changes that had occurred. This meant that they were more willing to include the press office in important senior-level discussions. There was growing recognition among officers that there is a need to effectively respond to the media and to engage with select stakeholder groups; the press office was a means by which to achieve these aims. This acceptance of the press office's significant role in contributing to shaping public perception and public opinion meant that direct access to the board was acquired.

POINTS FOR CONCLUSION

This was a very brief run-through of the communication strategies and programmes which the College undertakes through its press office. A further mark of success of the previous two years is the expansion of the press office's communications remit to include promotional work in international development issues on behalf of the College's International Office, which seeks to help under-resourced countries lower their maternal and newborn death rates.

This leads us back to the CIPR's definition of public relations given at the start of this case. Press office work is demanding and covers a range of communications and managerial functions when practised in a professional body or trade association. Depending on the organization, the environment in which it operates and its stakeholders, it may be useful to ensure that communications work includes policy and public affairs as in some cases the direction of policy and legislation will inform and steer communications activity.

In closing, it may be worthwhile to extend the CIPR's definition in the context of media relations to include: who you say it to (i.e. targeting your stakeholders) and how you go about saying what you need to say (i.e. the communications techniques and channels used).

8

Managing the evolution of an agency to meet the needs of a digital media environment

ROB BROWN

INTRODUCTION AND BACKGROUND

The impact of the internet on the dissemination of news and on both the structure and operation of the news media has been considerable. It was starting to become apparent by the middle of the first decade of the new millennium that wholesale and irreversible changes were happening. As the public relations industry had always functioned at least in part as an intermediary between various types of organizations and the media, these changes would inevitably impact on how public relations was to be conducted and how agencies should operate.

In April 2008, I returned to Staniforth, the PR agency at which I had first worked after graduating, as Managing Director. The business had been founded as Staniforth Williams, by journalists Phil Staniforth and John Williams, almost 30 years earlier in Manchester. A second office opened in London after 15 years. Many of the principles behind the way that the agency worked were drawn from newspaper newsrooms and throughout its history Staniforth had recruited journalists into the business. The agency continued to provide traditional public relations and press office services to some of the most respected businesses in the UK. Long-standing clients included Marks and Spencer, Aviva (formerly Norwich Union) and Nissan UK. It was clear to the management team that in order to remain competitive, the business would have to evolve.

CONTEXTUAL AND BENCHMARKING RESEARCH

While not strictly speaking a trailblazer in what some people were starting to call 'the new PR', the business sought to be a very early adopter of the new techniques and practices. Relatively few public relations agencies were making any outward changes to the way in which they operated.

Some of the clear examples of PR businesses that were re-evaluating their models were to be found in the United States. For a period, the changes that were taking place in the industry were collectively described using the term 'PR 2.0'. This term was a deliberate echo of the term 'web 2.0', which has been adopted by many to describe the iteration of the world wide web that has become socialized and increasingly populated by user generated content (UGC). Although UGC had been around in one form or another for many years, the arrival of social networking and so-called 'social media' made it commonplace.

A medium-sized agency in the United States called Shift Communications created the 'PR 2.0 Essentials' guide to educate its own staff about the growing range of social media tools. The guide, which examined a broad range of social media innovations, had been made freely available by Shift Communications to assist PR professionals in understanding the changes that were taking place within the industry.

Members of the senior team at Staniforth closely examined the published views of the principal at Shift Communications, Todd Defren and other leading proponents of PR 2.0 in the United States, like Brian Solis, author of the PR 2.0 blog and the principal at Futureworks PR. Of the larger global PR agencies, Edelman has been one of the pioneers in this arena. It was clear that the company was transferring skills acquired in the US market to its UK and European operations. Weber Shandwick, the world's largest global public relations firm, was also reshaping its offer in the US and the UK to accommodate the growing importance of digital communications.

GOALS AND OBJECTIVES

The principal objective was to evolve the agency to a point at which its staff had the knowledge and capability to deliver public relations programmes that took full account of the opportunities provided by the broader digital media. There were a number of specific areas of expertise that required particular focus:

- knowledge of the new digital channels;
- ability to evaluate the impact and importance of different web channels;
- understanding of the particular significance of content in an environment where impact will be related to the value of content;
- blogging skills and the ability to provide written content;
- expertise in editorial-driven search engine optimization (SEO);
- understanding and experience in the use of analytic tools (primarily Google Analytics).

A further goal was to provide an increased online presence for the agency. This would be important not just as part of the agency's own marketing and communications, but also as a means of validating our capability to the outside world. In an increasingly competitive public relations sector many agencies would offer digital PR and a portfolio of new products and services. Prospective clients would be bound to look online for evidence that agencies were able to practise what they preached. In this instance it would be necessary to avoid the 'cobblers' shoes' predicament.

STRATEGY

The programme would clearly require training, so a planned and sustained programme of staff training sessions would be a core element the activity. It would also be necessary to provide opportunities for the staff in the agency to have hands-on experience of blogging in order to practise the appropriate skills and techniques.

Creating an agency-published blog would therefore also be an important element of the programme. Using the blog would not only help people develop the required writing and content skills. It would also be a useful way of monitoring and examining how different techniques in headlining, writing, tagging and categorization impacted driving web traffic. It would allow us to do these things in a controlled and largely risk free environment. Having an agency blog would also give us a web presence that the agency owned and into which web analytics could be built, providing the opportunity for staff to play with and get to know the workings of Google Analytics and to measure cause and effect on the web in real time. Finally, the blog would also afford us the opportunity of getting to understand the relationship between editorial-based web content and search.

TARGET AUDIENCES

The target audiences for the program were both internal and external. The internal audience was clearly the most important because only through employees' commitment to acquiring and using new knowledge and skills would the programme achieve its objectives.

The external audience was secondary. It comprised existing clients, prospective or potential new clients and, to a certain extent, the marketing media. The long-term goal would be to make all of these audiences aware of the agency's capability in the digital environment. There was also an important short-term consideration. The concept of the internet, particularly in its present socialized form, means that almost everything an organization does is or has the potential to be in public. This would mean that the agency blog that was conceived to a large extent as a training school, would from the outset be visible as an external facet of the business. This was entirely unavoidable because if it was to function properly as a sandbox, it needed to generate real traffic in order to give the hands-on experience it was created to provide. It would mean, however, that certain quality controls would be essential from the outset. Although, if the programme was to be effective, these quality controls would have to be sufficiently flexible to allow freedom of use and therefore, in some cases, the freedom to make mistakes.

THE DELIVERY OF THE PROGRAMME

Staniforth commissioned the production of blog on the industry standard of the Wordpress platform. It was easy to use but sophisticated enough to have been used by major organizations like the *New York Times* and Playstation. The platform allowed all of the images, content and most aspects of the layout to be easily adaptable and therefore the entire blog would be managed directly by the contributors (i.e. the agency staff).

The blog was named 'PR Media Blog' in order to give it a somewhat independent feel. This was considered to be important because at the time corporate blogs were relatively uncommon and there was a certain amount of opposition on the web to corporate blogs that were overtly commercial. We wanted, however, to be clear that this blog was published by the agency. This information was provided in the 'About' section of the blog. After a couple of months, we felt sufficiently confident to add a discreet company logo to the front page with the statement 'Powered by Staniforth'. The other reason for choosing the name PR Media Blog is that the title of any website is important in terms of search. As the blog was going to be used for developing editorial-based search engine optimization techniques, it was hoped that after a reasonable time in operation the blog itself would rank highly in relevant searches.

At launch in April 2008, the content was provided by just two members of staff; this was doubled to four after a couple of months; by the six-month-mark, participation was widened to allow any member of staff to participate. Publishing rights were granted to all senior management team members. These rights allowed them to publish their own posts directly and without reference to anybody else in the agency. This also gave them the right to approve posts written by any of their team members. The guiding principle was that this should be collection of individual view points rather than an approved, agency point of view. This was important both to promote participation and to avoid the somewhat anodyne nature of the content that characterizes many corporate publications. All members of the agency were actively encouraged to blog. In almost every case, their unedited content is uploaded.

While contributors would be free to decide what content they wished to post, there would be some clear guidelines. Fairly obviously, the topics would have to fall into the broad categories of PR and the media. It was also important that content was not directly promotional but gave a flavour of the agency's creativity and interests through posts that would engage a wide range of audiences.

The blog was intended to represent the creative output of the agency in a pure form. Over 95 per cent of the written content would be created by agency staff at all levels. Images would be commissioned or researched and uploaded by the staff. The range of subject matter has been exceptionally broad, from the use of social media in the US presidential election, its impact on fashion and where designers like Marc Jacobs have harnessed some of its techniques through to observations on the Apollo moon landings.

In order to add to the wider interest, a number of guest bloggers, including the best selling US PR and marketing author David Meerman Scott, author of the best-selling *New Rules of Marketing and PR* and the digital media strategy adviser to Barack Obama, Thomas Gensemer of the Blue State Digital agency, were invited to contribute.

Engaging with organizations such as the Social Media Café Manchester – both online and offline – has built links with other bloggers helped to raise the profile and standing of PR Media Blog within the social media community.

Traffic to the site was driven in part by the highly dynamic nature of the content; new blog posts are added at an average rate of one to five per week. In addition, Staniforth set up a twitter feed to deliver RSS feeds for the blog. The feed is not in any way interactive; it simply acts to deliver headlines and links every time a new item is posted to the site.The twitter feed has grown entirely organically (i.e. there has been no follower strategy) to over 2,000 followers, a level which puts @PRMediaBlog in the top one percent of twitter feeds.

The staff were encouraged to use Google Analytics. This allows contributors to track visitor numbers and demographics with the ability to drill down deeply into the data and discover not just the levels of traffic for particular posts, but also how visitors discover the site (i.e. through twitter, links on other websites and blogs or search engines). In many cases, Google Analytics, using visitor IP addresses, also tells contributors who visits the site. This allows them to fully understand the process of how the content appeals directly to visitors to the blog.

By using Google Analytics to monitor and evaluate how users find and use the site, the agency was able to interpret the findings and hone content that over time allowed us to improve the blog's Google rank and increase visitor numbers.

Providing the staff with the tools with which to actively engage and learn for themselves about new channels and new techniques was a vital part of a programme, but it was not sufficient in itself. The agency introduced a six-month training pro-gramme under the banner of the 'Staniforth Academy'. This included an intensive 'Digiweek' session which included five consecutive days of intensive two-hour sessions focused solely on digital PR communications. The programme was of a standard that it was subsequently used by both a major UK retailer and a leading NHS body as the basis for training their own in-house PR and corporate communications staff.

A key element of the training was to teach the staff how existing public relations skills could be directly translated into highly relevant new ones (e.g. the importance of well written, lively, interesting and relevant copy and the fact that engaging content can have a direct impact on search engine rankings and, consequently, on traffic). Crafting words is a core skill for the majority of PR people and words still lie at the heart of modern PR just as much as they have always.

RESULTS AND EVALUATION

Some elements of the programme are far easier to measure than others. Many of the original objectives, the understanding of the significance of content, the development of blogging skills and the ability to provide that written content, along with the expertise in editorial-driven SEO and the ability to use of analytic tools, can be assessed via the highly measurable performance of the agency blog.

Within less than a year of operation PR Media Blog achieved a visitor level of around 10,000 per month. Put into context, that is more than ten times the number of people that visit the agency's more conventional website (www.staniforth.co.uk). Within just over six months the blog had started performing exceptionally well in search. Entering the term 'PR Blog' into Google would produce hundreds of millions of results, with the agency blog being consistently returned at the number one position. A similar search on the terms 'media' and 'blog' would see the agency site consistently in the top three returns on the front page of a Google search.

In July 2009, leading PR industry media intelligence services provider Cision published its top ten UK PR Blogs. It described the list as the most visible, engaged and social of the UK PR blogosphere. On their rankings PR Media Blog was number two in the UK.

The objectives of delivering knowledge of the new digital channels and the ability to assess the impact and importance of these various web channels are more difficult to evaluate. While somewhat anecdotal in nature we have been able to make some observations. The majority of the agency staff are actively using social networks as part of their daily routine (e.g. using twitter not just to monitor conversations relevant to clients and their communications programmes, but also as a way of directly engaging with journalists). The use of digital channels in a fully integrated way with other media has also become commonplace within the business. In addition, the agency has been asked to share its digital expertise with the Chartered Institute of Public Relations (CIPR) and has also provided training in this area for a number of in house communications teams.

UPDATE

In some ways this programme was entered into in order to transform Staniforth from one kind of an agency into another kind of an agency which is better suited to meet the communications requirements of a new era. This, however, could never be a finite process within a defined end point. The evolution of the medium is a constant process, therefore the practice of PR must also be under constant review and development.

One of many things that became apparent during the delivery of the programme was the astonishing speed at which new methods and tools for evaluating activity on the social web were emerging. At the start of the programme in the early part of 2008, there were few, if any, tools other than Google (and the myriad of other less popular but still fairly conventional search engines) that could be easily utilized for discovering and analyzing web content. These were not particularly good at discovering where dynamic conversations were taking place. However, this has changed significantly. The emergence of twitter and the availability of the programming code (i.e. the open application programming interface (API)) meant that developers created a myriad of tools for sifting through and organizing the huge volume of data supplied by twitter users. Not long after we had become empowered to search through twitter data for information, free tools (and tools available for purchase) that allowed us to search, collect and organize information from the whole gamut of blogs, forums, wikis and web communities became available. A new and more sophisticated form of media monitoring had emerged.

LESSONS

The key learning was that redefining the nature of the services that an agency provides should be a constant process. It can be accelerated or temporarily put on hold. However, if ignored for any length of time, it will impact business effectiveness and the relevance and usefulness of the products and services that the agency provides. Another important discovery was that if you want to change the way that a business operates, you have to take particular account of the individuals within that business. They will have differing desires for change and different capacities for making those changes. It is essential to allow people to develop at different speeds and to provide them with as many opportunities and tools as possible to learn and experience for themselves.

9

John Smith's 'The People's Franchise'

John Smith's People's Race and John Smith's People's Darts

TOM EARL

John Smith's is the UK's leading ale brand, selling over one million pints a day. The brand has steadily its grown market share in a declining category. It is now entering the sixth year of its Grand National sponsorship and, with virtually no TV advertising for the brand in the last two years, it currently relies on sponsorship PR as its key driver for media exposure.

The business objectives of the overall PR campaign are as follows:

1. Increase awareness of John Smith's sponsorships among ale drinkers in the UK.
2. Grow market share for the brand. Ale is a declining market but John Smith's aim is to reinforce their power brand credentials.
3. Engage with customers – 'Ordinary People Doing Extraordinary Things'.
4. Generate potential for sales promotions and display (off-trade) and increase sales volumes (on and off-trade).

In 2006, two years into their initial three-year deal as sponsor of the Grand National horse race at Aintree, John Smith's outlined their new objective of extending the 'campaignability' of their Grand National sponsorship and underlining their commitment as the biggest sponsor of UK horse racing. The brand team, along with SBI and Steam (their creative agency), were tasked with creating a strategy which delivered the following:

- 'campaignability' – provide a narrative throughout the winter to culminate in the Grand National in April for seven months of activity and coverage.
- brand positioning – John Smith's is the People's Pint and the Grand National is known as the People's Race.

- customer engagement – reinforce their key theme of 'Ordinary People Doing Extraordinary Things', take racing beyond the traditional sports media and create human interest stories.
- regional focus – selection of short-listed riders is aimed to ensure regional spread, therefore guaranteeing media buy-in across the country (something that the Grand National itself cannot always generate).

JOHN SMITH'S PEOPLE'S RACE

The solution was a charity flat race on Grand National day where ten ordinary members of the public are able to ride in front of a packed crowd at Aintree and millions on TV. It has become John Smith's single biggest investment in leveraging their sponsorship of the Grand National. The first three years have brought hugely beneficial results. Years two and three of the John Smith's People's Race have built on the great success of the first race in 2007 and 'Ordinary People Doing Extraordinary Things' has become central to the brand's DNA. The three years to date have seen a selection of teachers, nurses, farmers, surveyors, shepherds, students, delivery drivers and nail technicians given the opportunity to learn new skills and compete on the biggest stage imaginable. A jeweller from Droitwich won the 2009 race, following the success of an accountant from Newmarket and a pawn broker from Bournemouth.

Figure 9.1 People's Race logo

Campaign phasing

The John Smith's People's Race campaign sees concerted activity across three key phases: recruitment, training and the race. SBI, in conjunction with John Smith's and Aintree racecourse, have developed the concept in the following way:

Recruitment

Entries are driven by a major PR campaign which is based around previous riders, charity stories and the potential for a once in a lifetime opportunity. While regional media is the primary focus, the race receives considerable coverage across national press, with the majority coming via an award-winning media partnership with the *Daily Mirror*. SBI recruited Clare Balding, a leading BBC presenter, as an ambassador for the first two years of the campaign. In 2008–09 she was joined by Mick Fitzgerald, a recently retired Grand National and Gold Cup winning jockey. As an expert mentor, he was employed to prepare the riders for the challenges they were to face. The John Smith's People's Race has succeeded in taking racing beyond the traditional sports media and over 10,000 entries have been received to date.

In October 2008, the third People's Race was launched at Aintree racecourse. Interviews with the two John Smith's ambassadors and race sponsorship on the day generated extensive coverage, including BBC TV, Racing UK, *Liverpool Echo*, local TV and selected consumer media.

December 2008 saw the selection day at Tadcaster Brewery, the home of John Smith's. Thirty-two riders (four from each of the eight regions) from all walks of life were given the chance to progress to the next training stage. This gave SBI 32 separate opportunities to promote the race.

Training

To allay any potential fears about fitness and riding skills, the 2009 riders faced a more demanding training schedule. The 32 riders were split into northern and southern teams and based at the Northern Racing College in Doncaster and the British Racing School in Newmarket. Two intensive weekends enabled the expert coaches to reduce the group to a final 16. The final 16 went through to the next part of the training process.

Each of the riders was then allocated a professional trainer to provide them with the chance to hone their skills and get up to full racing fitness through riding out on their gallops at least three or four times a week. Some of the very best trainers in the country have been involved thus far, including Paul Nicholls, Nicky Henderson, Alan King and Jonjo O'Neill.

While conscious of the media interest in access to some of the top training establishments, SBI need to carefully manage the press activity at this stage to ensure the maximum coverage and the minimum of disruption to the trainers and their horses. In 2009, we hosted specific media days at each yard and encouraged journalists to attend on our terms. All trainers appreciate the need to promote the sport of racing as well as the benefits of promoting their own stable in the local media. Trainers are happy to participate despite receiving no fee to do so.

The riders also appeared in promotional events at their local pubs to publicize the John Smith's People's Race and to drum up local support. They also benefit from a visit to Warwick racecourse for a behind-the-scenes look at a race meeting; this provides a further media opportunity and the *Racing Post* has covered this event for the last two years.

Two to three weeks before the Grand National, the 16 riders face the final selection weekend. In a deliberately reality-style format, the riders face a panel of judges who select the Aintree Ten. Those selected possess the required skill, fitness and mental strength to face the challenge that the John Smith's People's Race presents. This took place at Southwell Racecourse last year and at the Northern Racing College this year with BBC cameras present. In 2009 we also arranged for a visit to The Plough, the pub managed by one of the riders, which is situated at the foot of the gallops used by trainer Jonjo O'Neill. This provided the setting for BBC's preview coverage.

The final element before the National week itself is the announcement of the ten horses that will run in the race. This usually follows shortly after the press releases detailing the ten riders and allows SBI to work closely with a betting partner (Ladbrokes in first two years and Coral in the third year) to target the racing press and promote the race as a betting medium.

The race

All ten riders are invited to Aintree on the Thursday or Friday of Grand National Week to provide interviews to the BBC, Racing UK and syndicated radio, to speak at various hospitality functions and to basically get a feel of what they can expect on the Saturday.

BBC Radio 5 host a live evening at Liverpool's Cavern Club on the Friday and SBI have always played a close part in managing this event. Two of the riders, including the Publican from Gloucestershire, were interviewed on this occasion, along with Mick Fitzgerald. They gave the listeners a good idea of what pressures they were facing with less than 24 hours to go!

On the Saturday morning – Grand National Day – walking the course at Aintree provides an additional opportunity for media to interview the riders, with SBI fielding calls from numerous radio stations and providing the group for TV interviews from the track.

BBC cover the build-up and the race during their broadcast on the Friday and Saturday, as well as televising the trophy presentation and interviewing the winning rider.

Media partnership

An award-winning partnership was developed with the *Daily Mirror* and the *Daily Record* (Media Week Awards 2007).

Their editorial teams worked closely with SBI and the commercial departments to produce a campaign. Recruitment was launched with a four-page pull-out and

Figure 9.2 People's Race jockeys

followed up with a series of advertorials building up to the race. This was complemented by in-depth coverage on the *Daily Mirror*'s website, which featured short video
documentaries, rider diaries and expert opinions. One journalist was designated
'Official People's Race correspondent', delivering more than ten pages of editorial
and a regular blog. John Smith's had six months of joined-up coverage ahead of the
three-day Grand National meeting, which went far beyond a paid solution. This
project now receives genuine editorial support, which is frequently so difficult to
deliver. The John Smith's People's Race provides a fantastic example of how it can be
done.

> It is a brilliant concept and a unique opportunity for *Mirror* readers to be a part of
> the greatest horse race in the world. We are already excited about the build-up to
> the 2010 People's Race next year.
>
> Dean Morse, Sports Editor, *Daily Mirror*

Charity

Charity is an extremely important component of the People's Race, with over
£100,000 being raised each year. Each rider selects a charity close to their own heart;
Direct Aid for Africa, Air Ambulance and the Injured Jockey's Fund have received
considerable sums of money to date. The betting partners also donate their takings
to charity. SBI also negotiated an official relationship with Sport Relief 08, whereby
John Smith's became the horse racing partner and raised money in pubs, clubs and
bars through sweepstake kits and race nights.

Figure 9.3 Charity donation

Campaign results

Overview: BBC and key media

The race has become an increasingly important part of BBC's Aintree coverage. The event is now known across a broad spectrum of national and regional sports, lifestyle and general consumer media.

Extensive coverage has included: BBC (Sport, Breakfast, regional stations, World Service, online, Sport Relief), Radio 5 Live, Talk Sport, Sky (sport and news), national print (*Telegraph*, *Times*, *Mirror*, *Mail*), Racing UK and over 170 regional radio stations and newspapers.

Research and results for 2008 race

Full evaluation results for the 2009 race were not available at the time of writing. However, results for the 2008 race were:

- 51 per cent of key consumers associate John Smith's with racing (up 7 per cent on 2007).
- There was 39 per cent awareness of People's Race (up 10 per cent on 2007)
- Advertising equivalent value gained through John Smith's People's Race over £2.8 million up 100 per cent (£1.4 million) on first year of race (FLE) ROI 10:1.
- There was a 32 per cent increase in brand/market share during the campaign (up from 26 per cent in 2007).
- There was a 43 per cent increase off-trade sales (up from 2006).
- £179,950 was raised for the Sport Relief charity (plus £101,000 for riders' chosen charities).
- It has won ISP Gold, Media Week and Marketing Excellence awards and been short-listed for many others.

(Millward Brown, 2008)

DEVELOPMENT OF THE JOHN SMITH'S PEOPLE'S FRANCHISE

In summer 2008, with the third People's Race already underway, it was agreed that 'Ordinary People Doing Extraordinary Things' should become increasingly central to John's Smith's marketing armoury, adding an aspirational but grounded element to the brand.

As a result, SBI helped develop the John Smith's 'People's' franchise with the addition of the John Smith's People's Darts, tying into John Smith's sponsorship of the BDO World Darts Championship (BBC TV).

JOHN SMITH'S PEOPLES DARTS 2009

John Smith's has established itself as a significant supporter of professional and grass-roots darts in less than 12 months.

As a result of powerful and truly innovative activation of this sponsorship in off-licences and other sales outlets, brewers Scottish and Newcastle (S&N) achieved significant incremental sales.

The campaign

John Smith's identified three key drivers of a successful event.

Sponsorship: BDO Lakeside World Professional Darts Championships/BDO Winmau World Masters

John Smith's is the official partner of these events. This partnership gives the brand pouring rights at the venue, branding opportunities at the venue and logo placements on players' shirts. The sponsorship secured the right to hold a darts tournament on the main stage at Lakeside and the venue's assistance in generating BBC coverage.

Darts ambassadors

Bobby George, BBC presenter and darts legend, was signed up as the face of People's Darts. Bobby has worked for John Smith's (and previously Courage) for many years and embodies the spirit of the campaign. SBI also recruited four current players, all of whom had previously won the World Championships: Martin Adams, John Walton, Ted Hankey and Mark Webster.

Media engagement

For launch activity, John Smith's engaged with trade press (*Club Mirror*, with a readership of 45,000 and *The Publican*, with a readership of 40,000) and consumer press (*Daily Mirror*). SBI also developed the partnership with BBC and their production agency TWI to cover the event from the launch onwards.

The events

Following the media launch, over 3,000 on-trade stockists ran qualifying tournaments in August and September 2008. Each venue providing a local champion to progress through to the regional finals. John Smith's provided kits and point-of-sale materials for each outlet.

Regional finals

The eight finals were used as local media opportunities, promotional events for John Smith's and chances for local darts fans to meet and play against world champions. Each mentor attended one regional final, playing against some of the contestants, speaking to various journalists and presenting the prizes.

The eight finalists who qualified through the regional finals were then provided with advice and tuition from one of the People's Darts mentors in the build-up to Lakeside. This included an evening at their pub or club – an event of considerable value to the venue as it is effectively an exhibition night as well as an event for the local media and the BBC cameras. The highlights included Bobby George's ferry trip to Argyll in the highlands of Scotland and an interview on Scarborough beach.

The finals at Lakeside

The final eight players and guests were invited to Lakeside to play the quarter- and semi-finals on the famous stage on the Tuesday afternoon. All of their mentors, plus a large crowd of friends and supporters, were there to cheer them on in front of the cameras.

The agreement with Lakeside to use their stage was crucial in facilitating over an hour of coverage on the BBC. The BBC spliced human interest pieces from the build-up into the darts action.

The final was played as the curtain raiser to the BDO World Championships in front of a full house at Lakeside. The BBC filmed this event and showed it during the interval of the World Final, which had 4.5 million viewers. Throughout the week, John Smith's achieved numerous verbal mentions as sponsor of both the World Championships and the People's Darts activity.

There was a total charity prize fund of £23,500. The winner also received a £2,500 sponsorship to play in three BDO tournaments including, the Torremolinos Open, and a pass into the qualifying rounds of the 2009 BDO Winmau World Masters.

Results

Key results from the first year of the John Smith's People's Darts activation are detailed below:

- The JSPD TV value alone has been estimated at over £500,000, with a collective PR value of well over £1 million.
- 'No Nonsense' associations with the John Smith's brand (as measured by Millward Brown) immediately after the activation of this sponsorship returned to previously established levels. (Data has not yet been published to measure the effect of the TV coverage.)
- John Smith's was heavily promoted as a key supporter of grass roots darts via the BBC, BDO and in outlet 'People's Darts' activation. The brand has also invested in providing John Smith's branded darts equipment for pubs and clubs throughout the UK.
- The brand was able to use a more humorous approach to its communication through the darts platform. The brand worked closely with its PR agency, the *Daily Mirror* and the professional mentors to establish the tone of voice that this activity would use. Humour associations with John Smith's also returned to previously established levels. (Data for TV coverage not available yet.)
- Over 23,000 people played the John Smith's branded darts game.
- The two shirt sponsorships were seen by over 12 million viewers. The final on 11 January 2009 peaked at over 4.5 million viewers.
- The JSPD BBC coverage was seen by an average of 718,500 people per ten minute segment, which is an impressive return for daytime.
- John Smith's achieved significant editorial support from the *Daily Mirror*, substantially over and above the paid advertorial.
- In the promotional period, an additional 350,000 pints of S&N supplied product were sold in the participating outlets. This equates to over £885,000 in additional turnover for these venues (at an average of approximately £2.50 per pint).
- According to Millward Brown, John Smith's saw a significant uplift in *claimed* TV awareness during the period of this activation. There was no other John Smith's

activity during this time. This brought claimed awareness back to levels last seen during John Smith's TV advertising.

- Over 8,000 readers of the *Daily Mirror* applied via www.johnsmiths.co.uk to claim their 'Free (Darts) Flights'. Most of these requested further information relating to next year's events.

SUMMARY

The John Smith's People's Race and People's Darts have quickly become established as news worthy events in their own right. They generated media value which was on brand equity and exceeded total investment in media by over 10:1.

The effective integration of all elements of the marketing and communications mix, combined with outstanding teamwork, delivers a significant uplift in awareness in John Smith's target audience.

10

Remembering The Few

GEOFF SIMPSON

INTRODUCTION

In 1940 a German invasion of Britain was a distinct possibility. Before any modern invasion can take place, the aggressor must achieve local air dominance. The Germans failed to do this. Many people acted heroically in averting the threat, but at the forefront were the Royal Air Force Fighter Command aircrew members, who achieved a 'unique and legendary place in the historiography of the war'.[1]

They became known as 'The Few' following a reference to them by then Prime Minister Winston Churchill in the House of Commons on 20 August 1940.

The National Memorial to 'The Few' is at Capel-le-Ferne on the cliffs between Folkestone and Dover in Kent. It was unveiled in 1993 by Her Late Majesty Queen Elizabeth the Queen Mother. The memorial was created and subsequently administered and maintained by a registered charity, the Battle of Britain Memorial Trust (BBMT), which receives no government or other official funding. The centrepiece of the memorial is a statue of a seated airman looking out to sea.

After the interest generated by the royal opening, the memorial received little publicity with the inevitable negative impact on public awareness and donations.

In 1999 the Trustees invited an experienced public relations practitioner, who happened to have an interest in the Battle of Britain, to provide pro bono advice to the Trust. At the time, a key issue was the approaching sixtieth anniversary of the Battle, which would generate many commemorative events and much media coverage.

RESEARCH

There were no funds available to undertake specific research.

The anecdotal evidence suggested that:

- With the generation who had lived through the Second World War in old age and many younger people ignorant of, or indifferent to, what had occurred, there was a danger that the memorial would come to be seen more and more as irrelevant.

- The opportunity existed to capitalize on the sixtieth anniversary and to maintain the momentum that it created.
- However, there was a specific threat in that there were plans by another body to create a London monument to The Few. While the approach of this other body, the Battle of Britain Historical Society (BBHS), was unsophisticated, the success that it was achieving through emotional appeals and the benefit of having a specific target, rather than maintaining an existing structure, could affect the ability of the BBMT to raise funds for maintenance of the National Memorial. There was also a persuasive argument that London, the country's capital, should have a Battle of Britain monument, particularly as much aerial fighting had taken place over London.

GOALS AND OBJECTIVES

The goals and objectives follow:

1. Establish, with decision takers, opinion formers and in the public mind the importance of the Battle of Britain in the country's history (thus fulfilling the educational remit, which has been part of the Trust's objectives since it was established).
2. Encourage donations, particularly substantial ones, that would ensure that the memorial remains for all time as a reminder of the events of 1940.
3. Encourage interest in the memorial from people too young to remember the Second World War.
4. Encourage the public to visit the memorial and its site.
5. Stress the appropriate setting of the National Memorial in an area of the country over which much fighting had occurred.
6. Stress the empathy of the BBMT with the veterans of the conflict, their exclusive organizations, the Battle of Britain Fighter Association (BBFA), other ex-service bodies and the Royal Air Force.
7. Maintain the interest in the Battle and the National Memorial beyond the sixtieth anniversary year.

COMMUNICATION STRATEGY

The plan that was presented to and agreed by the Trustees envisaged utilizing a limited budget by placing heavy emphasis on a professional media relations campaign. The BBMT would become a source of authoritative information on 1940 and would be available to the media 24 hours a day, seven days a week. The goodwill and trust that this would create would make journalists more ready to receive approaches from the Trust and to consider material submitted. At all times the surviving veterans and the memory of those who had given their lives would be treated with great respect.

It was felt important to stress the strengths of the BBMT. Although donations were needed, the organization was financially sound and responsible in the way it dealt with money. Trustees included senior retired RAF officers and major figures in the business world.

It was important to stress that this was the National Memorial to The Few. At the same time, emphasis needed to be placed on the pride which the BBMT felt in its association with the County of Kent.

All opportunities should be taken to associate the memorial with both the veterans of the Battle and younger generations.

All responses to the media and material written for publication would be tested against these points.

TARGET AUDIENCES

Key audiences were determined as:

1) decision makers and opinion formers (national, regional and in the service community);
2) companies and individuals who are in a position to make significant donations;
3) the general public who might visit the memorial and support it financially through donations and the purchase of souvenirs;
4) people born after 1945.

THE CAMPAIGN

The first move, in 1999, was to issue to a wide range of journalists a 'basic guide' to the Battle of Britain The guide had the phone numbers of the public relations consultant and offered an immediate response to enquiries. This was immediately successful. It was helped by the consultant's knowledge of the Battle and the willingness of BBMT's President, Chairman, Secretary and other trustees to play their part in the campaign.

Links were established with RAF Corporate Communications (as it was then called) at the Ministry of Defence.

A series of media releases was issued in the run up to the start of commemorative events in the summer of 2000 and, especially, the annual Memorial Day at the memorial, which marked the anniversary of the start of the Battle in July. Coverage started to build up.

Invitations were issued to all relevant media to attend Memorial Day and associated events. Interviews were arranged with veterans. Stories were arranged including a meeting between a veteran who had been shot down into the sea in the Battle and the son of one of the lifeboatmen who had brought him to safety. Another former pilot was photographed with a man who, as a teenage farmhand, had been one of the first on the scene after the pilot had been injured in landing a damaged Hurricane fighter in a field near the memorial site.

Bringing together all the aircrew veterans, who were present, in front of a bank on which photographers could stand, provided an excellent photo opportunity. Veterans were also photographed talking to young people.

The RAF provided two officers to assist with the media. Various BBC, ITV and Sky crews, *The Times*, *Daily Telegraph*, *Sun*, Press Association and a number of local and regional newspapers attended and later covered the event. BBC Radio Kent broadcast from the site.

UPDATE

Since 2000, the media campaign has been maintained and developed. The basic guide has been updated and reissued from time to time. The ability to offer responses 24/7 has been kept in place. Frequent stories have been issued and exclusive news stories and features have been widely placed. Media work always reaches a climax at the time of Memorial Day in July, with a second peak around 15th September, the official Battle of Britain Day. Meetings with individual journalists are arranged regularly.

Opportunities have been taken to turn negatives into positives. For example, in 2007 a collecting box on the site was broken into and money was stolen. Local paper coverage was obtained, including photographs of the damaged box. Many people were disgusted at such action. The memorial's ongoing need for funds was highlighted.

The campaign has moved beyond media relations. For example:

- In late 2000, the BBMT launched The Friends of The Few, a support organization for the National Memorial. The several hundred members receive benefits including discounts on the cost of tickets for the guest marquee at Memorial Day and battlefield tours which are run each summer. Members also receive regular newsletters and an annual magazine, *1940*, which carries articles about the memorial and the events and personalities of the period.
- Receptions aimed at raising the profile of the memorial, as well as attracting large donations, have been held at Government House in Jersey and twice in the House of Commons with the support of Lord Graham of Edmonton PC. Individual presentations have also been made to potential donors.
- A guide to the memorial was published in 2005, with an updated edition appearing in 2008. This is sold to visitors, but it is also used as a brochure, when contact is being made with journalists, potential donors, etc.
- All trustees are encouraged to include their position with the BBMT in *Who's Who* entries and other reference works. A sponsorship brochure was produced in 2008 and has been widely circulated, with all trustees being asked to send copies to key contacts.
- In 2003 HRH Prince Michael of Kent agreed to become Patron of the BBMT. He has proved an assiduous supporter, attending events as often as possible.
- A new website was launched in 2006. It tells the story of the Battle and the memorial, announces forthcoming events and reports on those that have taken place and has a media section with contact numbers.
- Other profile-raising events have been organized. Perhaps the most notable is the 2008 Royal Gala concert that was held at the London Palladium in the presence

Figure 10.1 Programme cover

of Prince Michael. Stars including Robert Hardy, Nicholas Parsons, Millicent Martin, Celia Imrie, Diane Keen and Blake recreated the atmosphere of the 1940s for a packed house. Adding to the atmosphere was the presence of more stars in the audience. Richard Todd, who starred in such war-themed classic films as *The Dam Busters* and *The Longest Day* was instantly recognizable and much sought after. Virginia McKenna, who played the secret agent Violette Szabo GC in *Carve Her Name With Pride*, also attended and went on stage.

- Show business celebrities such as Sir Donald Sinden, Neil Pearson, Jan Leeming and Muriel Pavlow, a star of the films *Reach for the Sky* and *The Malta Story*, now regularly attend Memorial Day, adding to the public's attraction to the event.

- Through the enthusiastic support of the Air Training Corps – particularly the Kent Wing – youth plays an important and prominent part in Memorial Day and other events. Teenage cadets, supervised by their adult officers, act as car park attendants, sell programmes, shake collecting buckets, operate as runners and assist in various other ways. Pupils and staff from Capel-le-Ferne primary school join the commemoration on Memorial Day.

- Features have been added to the memorial site including full-sized replicas of Hurricane and Spitfire aircraft and, in 2005, the Christopher Foxley-Norris Memorial Wall on which the names of all the allied airmen who took part in the Battle are inscribed. The late Air Chief Marshal Foxley-Norris, a pilot in the Battle, was a great benefactor of the memorial, together with Lady Foxley-Norris, who continues as a dedicated supporter.

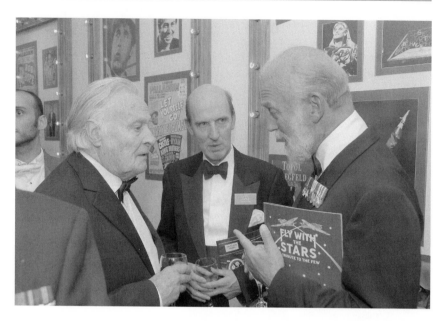

Figure 10.2 Prince Michael

RESULTS AND EVALUATION

The BBMT, a registered charity, has not been able to allocate funds for any structured system of evaluation. However, newspaper, magazine, radio, television and new media coverage has been collated and regularly analyzed for its impact and the manner in which it meets or fails to meet the agreed objectives. It is clear that the media's use of the key term 'National Memorial' has greatly increased.

There are many other matters which suggest the successful progress of the campaign.

For example:

- Shortly after the sixtieth anniversary of the Battle, the RAF officially recognized Memorial Day as an RAF event. The Chief of the Air Staff attends on a regular basis. The service supports other BBMT events too.
- Attendance at events, letters received and conversations held all indicate that the memorial is now better known.
- There is now considerable public interest in the Second World War generally and the Battle of Britain in particular. This is reflected, for instance, in the number of newspaper articles, broadcast programmes and specialist websites on the subject. The trustees have no doubt that the campaign has played its part in this.
- The BBMT has increasing interface with young people. They attend events, write asking for help with school projects and dissertations and attend talks given by trustees.

- It is clear that donations and legacies are now received from people who have come to know of the memorial through its increased profile.
- The separate campaign to raise funds for a London monument came to a conclusion in 2005, with the erection of that monument. The 'threat' has therefore passed with no significant impact on the ability of the BBMT to raise funds.
- Secondary publicity (i.e. where there has been no direct approach by the BBMT) now frequently occurs. For instance, a recent edition of the ordnance survey map (1: 50,000 scale) covering the locality of the memorial features a colour picture of the airman statue on its cover. Other maps, guidebooks and locally produced tourist information, now frequently refer to the memorial, as do blogs produced by walkers and people interested in military history. The memorial featured strongly in the 2006 novel *Blue Man Falling* by Frank Barnard.
- Frequent requests for information on the Battle, as well as the memorial, are received from journalists, authors and historians. These often lead to a BBMT credit.

THE FUTURE

The media campaign will continue indefinitely. There will be steady, but tasteful, development of the National Memorial site.

The BBMT will take full advantage of the opportunities offered by the seventieth anniversary of the Battle of Britain in 2010.

NOTE

1   For further information see J. Crang, Identifying the Few: the personalisation of a Heroic Military Elite, in *War and Society*, School of Hunamities and Social Sciences, The University of New South Wales, Australian Defence Force Academy, 2005, 24 (2) November 13–22.

11

When PR meets marketing

On the intraorganizational challenges in the implementation of integrated communication

SIMON TORP

INTRODUCTION

KMD is the largest Danish-owned information technology (IT) supplier and one of Denmark's largest providers of IT solutions to the public sector. KMD develops and provides IT solutions for the local authority, state and corporate markets. The company has 3,000 employees and an annual revenue of more than DKK 3 billion. On 1 January 2004 the company integrated its PR/communications and marketing departments, with the aim of moving towards an integrated communication function. This makes KMD an interesting case since the integration meant that all the staff employed in the communications and marketing departments now had to relate to each others' disciplines (see Appendix 11.1).

THEORETICAL BACKGROUND

Prior to the 1980s, marketing and PR were regarded as distinct functions with different objectives and target groups. In the 1980s, however, it was increasingly accepted that the two functions shared a number of common features while being at the same time complementary. This crucial change in thinking arose in part from the perception among some academics and practitioners that both marketing and PR could be fundamentally asymmetrical activities, whereas it had previously been claimed that PR was, or could be, an essentially symmetrical practice.[2] Because of this shift in perception, the practice of treating PR and marketing as two distinct functions, which in many companies operated quite independently of one another, has been increasingly abandoned in favour of a model in which the two functions would ideally be integrated, coordinated, aligned and in some cases completely fused. This ideal and the efforts to achieve it came to be known as 'integrated (marketing) communication'. Integrated communication can be defined as the notion and the practice of aligning symbols, messages, procedures and behaviours in order for an organization to communicate with consistency, coherence, clarity and continuity within and across formal organizational boundaries.[3]

THE ORGANIZATION: KMD BEFORE THE INTEGRATION

According to one of the managers within KMD, the extent of coordination between the communications department and the marketing department prior to the restructuring was comparable to that between North and South Korea: there was no cooperation. Another employee within the company described the relationship between the two departments as 'trench warfare'. On the basis of Hallahan's typology of possible relations between communications and marketing, the relationship between the communications department and the marketing department prior to the integration could best be described as combative. Under this type of relationship, communications and marketing view each other as opponents and compete for tasks and resources.[4] Likewise, the cooperation with external communications and marketing agencies was not integrated. The communications and marketing departments within KMD used different agencies and did not always internally integrate and coordinate the services that the agencies supplied in the individual departments. It was a situation of the kind Pickton and Broderick describe as 'anarchic structures'.[5]

Several people from the old communications department within the company implied that some of their colleagues deliberately tried to give the marketing department a bad reputation. According to the press officer, the impression was successfully created that the marketing department was not doing its job properly. Then, when the staff satisfaction survey once again clearly showed that the staff in marketing felt that their boss was incompetent as a manager – he received the worst

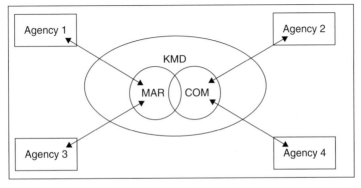

Before the integration

Figure 11.1 Before the integration

staff satisfaction rating of any manager in the company – the opportunity was seized to take over the marketing department. The head of sales could use the bad survey results as an argument for deposing the head of marketing and dissolving the marketing department as an independent unit.

According to the researcher Lauzen, there is a clear correlation between a manager's self-image and the probability of intervention or encroachment in relation to the unit managed. If the manager lacks sufficient skills to lead the department, it creates, according to Lauzen, a power vacuum and senior management will be urged to allow an external person (in a professional or functional sense) take over the role.[6] Lauzen's description matches well with the process in KMD, apart from the fact that Lauzen's research deals with relations and power struggles between communications and marketing, in which marketing plays the role of the aggressive and imperialistic party, while communications is in the role of the potential victim. At KMD, on the other hand, it was the other way around; here it was marketing that had a weak manager, and the manager of communications knew how to take advantage of this.

THE LITTLE FISH ATE THE BIG FISH: MERGER OR HOSTILE TAKEOVER?

The overwhelming majority of the employees from the old marketing department, and some employees in the old communications department viewed the integration of the two departments essentially as a case of the communications department taking over the marketing department. Several people described it as a hostile takeover or as the little fish eating the big fish, referring to the fact that in terms of the number of employees, the communications department was smaller than the marketing department. Some people said that the takeover had been wrapped in a transparent tissue of merger rhetoric which had merely made matters worse. They say that it would have been better if management had been more honest. Such honesty, would have reduced expectations to a more realistic level in relation to the degree of influence and the prioritization of tasks.

One of the staff from the old marketing department took a procedural perspective with regard to the question of whether the process was a merger or a takeover. She felt, and expressed the hope, that there will eventually be a movement from takeover to merger. 'This is not a merger yet, but I think it will be in time', she said. According to this member of staff, what will alter the character of the integration is improved familiarity. Once the former marketing and communications staff get to know each others' professional areas, staff will also learn to respect each other more, which will lead to the communications department staff and particularly the managers, recognizing marketing as an equal partner. The integration will thereby become less of a takeover and more of a merger.

According to theorist Hallahan, the takeover relationship typically occurs in companies where either marketing or communications has a stronger position than the other. It is thereby often the result of an unequal struggle between the two functions.[7] One of the decisive factors affecting the outcome of the struggle between the professional disciplines, according to Hallahan, is the strength and organizational location of the respective managers, which neatly matches the situation at KMD in advance of the integration of the communications and marketing departments.

THE ORGANIZATION: KMD AFTER THE INTEGRATION

How the general organization of communications and marketing in the new integrated department is described depends on whether you feel the process was a takeover or a merger. On the basis of Hallahan,[8] if the action was a takeover, the relationship might be illustrated as in Figure 11.2.

In the integration of the communications and marketing departments, the title of the senior manager in charge changed from being Director of Communications to Director of Communications and Marketing. To support cooperation in the new integrated department, open-plan offices were established. Only the managing director and a single hard-core smoker were allowed to remain in one-person offices. A number of project groups were established in connection with the integration of the departments. Most of these groups consisted of staff from both marketing and communications. The department was located in both Odense and Ballerup. In order to secure coherence in the work and enhance the sense of community spirit, so-called 'unit meetings' were held every 14 days. At these meetings, the managing director provided news from the management board, and representatives of the various project groups presented the results of their work.

INTEGRATED COMMUNICATION

If the integration of an organization's communication is to be realized effectively, according to the theorists Schultz and Kitchen, it is necessary that responsibility for all communications activities is centralized. A so-called communications 'tsar', who will be responsible for supervising all of the company's communications, must be appointed.[9] This idea also applies at KMD, where the press officer was assigned this

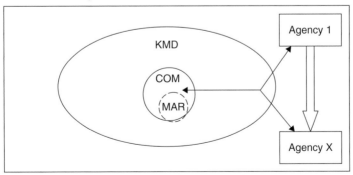

Figure 11.2 After the integration

role. He was appointed the 'responsible head' or editor-in-chief of all media communications, which, among other things, meant that the former editor-in-chief of print publications was degraded to editor. The objective of the centralization and the appointment of an editor-in-chief was to ensure that uniform or consistent messages appeared in all media. As an element in the centralization of control over communications, a committee was formed under the leadership of the editor-in-chief and press officer. This committee was described by one of its members as a 'super-editorial team'. It consisted of the editor-in-chief, the manager responsible for the intranet, the manager responsible for the internet, the manager responsible for the extranet or customer net and the editor of print publications. The designation of communications tsar was not used at KMD. The press officer is termed 'message manager' in the above-mentioned message documents, while in some emails he signed as 'message president'. The term the press officer's colleagues used for his new post was mainly 'editor-in-chief'. The management's intention was to secure greater uniformity in campaigns and materials. For this reason they limited the number of different agencies used and increased the level of supervision of all kinds of communication. If several external parties were involved in compiling the communication for any particular campaign project, it was up to the responsible manager at KMD to ensure that the tasks and services provided were in harmony with the line which had been laid down for the campaign and, where appropriate, in co-operation with an agency for messages and design.

MESSAGE MANAGEMENT: ONE VOICE OR MULTIPLE VOICES

One of the decisive motivations for integrating communication and marketing at KMD was the wish to be able to improve the supervision of the communications and the management of the messages. The alignment of messages is a key element in integrated communication. It is also a frequently used concept in the research.[10] Several of the senior employees seemed to subscribe to the idea that integrated communication should be completely synonymous with 'univocality' or 'one-voice'. As they saw it, integrated communication was a matter of saying the same thing to everyone, and doing so again and again, so as to be sure that anyone who thought about KMD would immediately associate it with one particular message: 'Efficient IT for the new Denmark'. For the press officer, one of the decisive advantages of integrated communication was that it enabled one to speak with greater strength, which he felt enhanced the possibility of being heard and getting one's message across:

> It's about giving you a bigger megaphone. Or if you like, many small megaphones are equivalent to one large one. One large megaphone is a lot more powerful than many small toots. We speak with greater strength, and there is consistency in our messages. We say the same thing everywhere, so there is a better chance of the messages being heard.

Several of the employees point out, however, in line with certain theorists[11], that such control of the company's messages does not necessarily exclude differentiation and diversity. According to one staff member, it was merely a question of securing a degree of uniformity and of saying the same thing in different ways or, as another person put it, marketing and communication must 'speak with the same authority'.

THE MESSAGE DOCUMENT

One of the tools KMD utilized to manage its communication was a so-called 'message document'. The message document is a tool that enables a company to work with messages which are simultaneously consistent and dynamic and consists of main messages, submessages and documentation.[12] The main messages, which comprise the essential messages that a company wishes to communicate to the surrounding world, should be constant over time. The submessages, which give reality to, support and harmonize the main messages, may, on the other hand, be adapted as necessary. The documentation, which might, for example, consist of various items of factual information used in connection with message communication, is the most dynamic and must be updated on an ongoing basis. The message document can form the basis of editorial plans in relation to customer magazines, staff newsletters, relations with the press, etc. At KMD, message documents were compiled in connection with the local government structural reform. According to the press officer, the advantages of being able to control your messages and show consistency can be explained with the help of a dating metaphor:

> [If] you want to have a girlfriend, you are assessed in all kinds of different ways. You are assessed by your family, the colour of your eyes, the way you smell, the way you dress, your performance in every way, right? And in the same way, a company is also assessed by its performance in all areas. But there is no doubt that if we have control over this, if we give the right impression, then we will inevitably have an effect. So you could say that if you perform really well on a date in all areas that suit the taste of the girl you are out with, then there is no doubt that it will create a better impression.

DESIGN

From a theoretical perspective, a very important factor when companies integrate their communication is the immediate impression created through their visual representation in terms of logos, typography, colours, types of pictures used, etc; it is a question of creating harmony between all the forms of visual articulation emanating from the organization. The aim is to create 'one look, one voice'[13] or 'one sight, one sound'.[14] At KMD, the visible part of the communication played a major role in the introduction of integrated communication to the company. In fact, according to the press officer, one of the arguments for integrating the communications and marketing departments in the first place was that this would make it easier to create a uniform expression and a high degree of recognition in all parts of the communication. A number of groups were formed to handle various areas in connection with the integration. One of these groups had the task of developing a new corporate visual identity (CVI)[15] and choosing the agency with whom this work would be done. The integration of a company's visual expression is often regarded as a relatively simple manoeuvre, but this is most certainly not always the case. We can see this from the example of KMD, where the work of compiling a new CVI turned out to be one of the most difficult and dramatic projects in the integration process. What at first glance might appear to be quite literally a superficial task revealed itself to be associated with such strong emotions that people became seriously agitated about it.

There was a great deal of disagreement concerning whether the external recipients of the company's communications (i.e.customers) should be consulted during the design process. Some people felt that various surveys should be carried out to determine how the recipients experienced different design lines and colours, so that selected designs and colours could be in conformity with the image that the company wished to project. These surveys, it was proposed, could take the form of focus group interviews or various tests. The marketing people were among the principal proponents for consultation with the recipients. However, this view was strongly opposed by the press officer and several people from communications. They felt that this would be a waste of time and money, as the company itself could easily determine what worked and, since the customers did not know 'whether they wish to be assaulted with blue or green or yellow', you could end up surveying the question to death. Asking the customers about this was, in the opinion of those who opposed it, tantamount to saying the company was incapable of assessing for itself how well its communication functioned. As the press officer put it, 'You don't ask your mother what you should wear tomorrow. We're not complete idiots!' When asked whether he felt that companies could become too uniform in their communication and design towards many different target groups, the press officer replied that a company could certainly choose to say:

> We are a rainbow company. We communicate in all the colours of the rainbow. Our design is yellow and blue and green, precisely because we communicate with the reality out there, which is very diverse. But instead, we just take a decision. We say that, if we need a mouthpiece, then it is more important for us to be visible with certain messages in this period, when we need to create an impact in relation to the message war that we are engaged in. So in design terms, we need to support these messages. If there was no such war going on, if we could act in isolation and did not need to position ourselves so much in relation to other companies, then we could communicate more on other people's terms.

The absence of end user surveys in connection with the formulation of messages and the choice of design is explained with reference to the fact that the company was engaged in a 'message war'. The company should not therefore attempt to reflect the diversity of its surroundings, but should rather be selective and unambiguous, if it is to make itself heard above the noise. The head of analysis, who had previously been responsible for the company's corporate design for many years, felt that it was important to undertake analyses of the preferences of the target groups. One of the reasons for this, in his opinion, was that the design people's view of design, in relation to such aspects as appearance and picture style, could often be completely out of step with the views of the customers. You become seduced by your own ideas and products, forgetting that the target group may be in a completely different world to that of you and your colleagues.[16]

INTEGRATED COMMUNICATION AS BEHAVIOUR

As stated in the introductory definition, integrated communication is not just about aligning messages and symbols; it can also encompass behaviour.[17] At KMD, the implementation of integrated communication meant that the identity of staff members was to be more closely linked to that of the company. Employees should act not as individuals, but as KMD staff, expressing the values of the company. The managing director expressed his hopes as follows:

> I suppose integrated communication is about getting the company to appear as a united whole outwardly. Not just in communication and marketing, but also through our sales staff. It is after all a KMD employee that you meet, in the sense that it is a person who expresses KMD's values, rather than just some John Smith or other who turns up, and who happens to work for KMD.

The communications should, he says, 'permeate' the company. This means that the company's messages and its values should be adopted and communicated by all of the players in the organization. The managing director was not the only one to have this vision; one of the regular staff stated that KMD should be the identifying point of all staff in the company. Other members of the integrated department emphasized the importance of having 'a common front and a common attitude' and that the company's employees should stop 'doing their own thing'. The problem, according to one member of staff, was not just that the company's employees went their own way, as mentioned by the managing director above, but also that they primarily identified with the company at the subcorporate level (i.e. the department or team). The staff at KMD did not only identify themselves in relation to the company or parts of it; some employees identified themselves first and foremost with players from outside the organization. According to a marketing expert from the department, the customer managers saw themselves primarily as the customer's representatives at KMD, rather than KMD's representatives to the customers. The focus of the press officer was directed first and foremost at communications centrally compiled and issued by the organization as he found it difficult to control such factors as the behaviour of the sales staff towards the customers. He apparently felt that by controlling the written materials and placards, and the messages expressed in these, he could encourage the employees to communicate in accordance with them, even when they were acting alone.

Within the research literature, too, the idea that integrated communication is not just about the superficial aspects of communication (e.g. design) but also about encompassing the ways of acting and thinking of the organizational players, is relatively widespread. Åberg, for example, states that one of the functions of communication is to turn organization members into good citizens of the organization.[18] This socialization process, it is claimed, is an essential element in the integration of the communicative processes in the organization. Another very clear example of this way of thinking is found in the book *Corporate Religion* by agency owner and communication consultant Jesper Kunde. The book states that in order to ensure that employees will express the values of the company, there should be compatibility, prior to hiring new employees, between the incoming staff member's values and the values and attitudes of the company.[19] If a company wishes to get its staff to integrate with the value universe of the company, it must ensure that they already have the right attitudes when they are join the company. Having the right 'religion', according to Kunde, should be a condition for being employed by the company in the first place.

Integrated communication can also encompass the behaviour of employees outside their work, with the private lives of staff members becoming more closely integrated than before with the company's value universe, and vice versa.[20] This, according to several employees, has also been the case at KMD. As one of the staff members who has been there longest puts it, the work has 'eaten its way into' the employees' lives. In her opinion, the private lives of employees have become more public, 'because it all has to be integrated'. It has become politically incorrect not to express a very open attitude:

> The work has also changed, because it eats its way into you. And you can quote me on that. It's not just at KMD. The way things are, you can hardly have a private life, because it all has to be integrated. Your workplace has to watch over you and make sure you have a good home life, check on what you eat, whether you smoke and so on. It's getting to the point where you can hardly get any peace anymore. There are certainly some people who feel that your private life just disappears. And if you're not very open and so on, you might be considered politically incorrect. Your private life has become more public.

Previously, this staff member never used to turn off the mobile phone she used at work; it was not necessary as no one would dream of calling her outside normal working hours. Now, people are expected to be available round the clock. She feels it is practically seen as an act of civil disobedience or rebellion against the new norms if she turns off her mobile phone in the time she spends outside KMD. She feels that this is because the company's demands on its employees have risen, as have the employees' demands towards themselves. The expression '24–7' is used at KMD to describe the expectations of managers and staff towards increased commitment and time consumption (i.e. people should be constantly available).

Another critical voice came from one of the youngest members of staff. She is also an opponent of the expanded working hours, such as when her colleagues take their mobile phones on holiday and check and reply to their emails while on holiday. This, she says, has created an unpleasant atmosphere because people are practically competing to show who is most available to KMD during what had otherwise been regarded as their leisure time. However, it is not just about being 'available 24 hours a day'. People are also very concerned about drawing attention to the fact that they are available. The 24–7 ideal does not just apply to the permanent employees, as student helpers are also expected to 'give their souls and leisure time' to the company. When directly asked whether there were any times when he did not think about KMD, the acting manager of the Odense branch of the communications department replied, 'They are certainly limited'.

INTEGRATED COMMUNICATION AS A SHARED VALUE COMMUNITY

Shortly after the integration of the marketing and communications functions was completed, a member of the HR department gave a presentation on the importance of consistency or harmony between the working lives and private lives of the organization and its employees. A staff member who had been head of the marketing team at the Odense branch prior to the integration of the former communications and marketing departments felt that there should be alignment between the personal values of the staff and the values of the company and the department. However, she also pointed out a challenge in relation to this attitude in that some staff members may have 'chosen KMD on the basis of values which are different to those now being applied'. By contrast, one of the ordinary employees expressed a clear rejection of the idea of harmony between the values of the company and the employees' personal values and did not support the concept of the boundaries between work and private life being completely eroded away:

> The idea that your personal values should support those of the company is in my opinion is a load of nonsense, and I don't think it can ever become a reality, neither here nor anywhere else. If anyone claims that to be the case, it isn't so. Naturally when you are working somewhere you would like to be able to support the things that the company stands for, but you also have a life outside of your work. I don't bloody well feel I'm a KMD staff member in my free time or anything like that.

According to this person, it is entirely possible to agree with what the company stands for without necessarily identifying with it in your leisure time. This staff member maintains in other words a clear distinction between work and leisure time. For her, the KMD identity is exclusively for work. On the basis of the above insights, one could conclude that there has been some increased tension between the company and its employees over the boundaries between their working and personal lives and values. These tensions are not necessarily the results of the implementation of integrated communication at KMD, but they have been accentuated in this connection. The 24–7 availability idea impinges on the boundary between working hours and leisure time. Other personal- and work-related boundaries that have been affected, as we have seen, include the boundary between the values of the company and personal values and the boundary between private life and working life. While the first two infringements reflect the fact that the company is encroaching in various respects on the private lives of its employees, the infringement of the boundary between the private sphere and the working sphere, as expressed by the expectation of greater openness in relation to private matters on the part of colleagues and managers, reflects a movement in the opposite direction. In this connection, there is an implicit demand that staff should (also) be prepared to involve their private lives in and at their work.

ZERO-BASED

Under integrated communication, tasks are solved in what the literature refers to as a 'zero-based' manner.[21] The concept of 'media-neutral planning' roughly describes the same efforts.[22] Zero-based means that problems and challenges are not defined purely on the basis of individual professional disciplines or channels as this can lead to the problem or task – and any potential solution – being defined on the basis of narrow professional interests. The fact that your perception of reality is determined by the professional hat you wear is sometimes popularly expressed in the saying 'to a man with a hammer, everything looks like a nail'. At KMD, zero-based work was an ideal aspired to by many of the staff. The establishment of working groups with both communications and marketing people was viewed by many regular staff members as an opportunity to work in a zero-based manner. Some staff members, however, saw it as part of the managing director's attempts to 'train' or 'control' the marketing and communications staff. One communications staff member who was intent on working across the boundaries of the disciplines, and thereby achieve synergy, expressed the following view of integrated communication:

> There are various professional disciplines, there is press work, crisis com-
> munication, internal communication, change communication and marketing. If
> you put all these things into a pot and stir well, then when a subject or a task comes
> along, you can take out the things you need to solve the task, and it doesn't matter
> which professional hat you are wearing, or what your educational background is;
> you form a project group with various competencies drawn from across the
> boundaries of the professional disciplines. And that means that you don't all have
> to possess the same skills, but you must all be capable of making use of each other
> and melding the competencies together. And when you do that, what you have is
> integrated communication.

MUTUAL VIEWS AND PREJUDICES

Marketing is a part of communication: the relationship between the disciplines seen from the communications perspective

One of the greatest challenges in connection with the realization of integrated communication at KMD consisted of the views and prejudices held by the communications and marketing people towards each other, and the consequent view of what the professional and practical relationship should be between the disciplines. The relations between the disciplines is also one of the current points of contention in connection with the integration of communication and marketing within the field generally, as it is critical to the understanding, expression and organization of integrated communication. Many theorists feel that integration will inevitably mean a hierarchical relation between the participating disciplines and that their own discipline, for both theoretical and practical reasons, should rightfully take the leading and strategic role.[23] This picture also applied at KMD.

According to the director of the new department, whose professional background was in communications, marketing is a communication discipline which is primarily aimed at customers, while communication in general is not limited in the same way, but is aimed at all stakeholders. An equivalent view was expressed by one of the other communications people; marketing, she said, is about communication. Communication is the overall discipline; marketing is one of several branches of communication. This view of marketing also influenced the full-page advertisement published by KMD in the Danish *Who's Who* for the communications branch in 2004. Under the heading 'The common element – integrated communication at KMD', the advertisment said: 'We cover all communication disciplines, including marketing.' Above the text were one large and two small photographs of five communications people. The wording of the advertisement, and the fact that only people from the old communications department were featured in the pictures were viewed by the marketing people in the department as an affront. The marketing people saw it as yet another sign of disrespect for them and their professional skills.

Communication is a part of marketing: the relationship between the disciplines seen from the marketing perspective

Naturally enough, the employees from the old marketing department did not share the view of the communications people that marketing is merely one of the disciplines of communication. For the marketing people, it was precisely the other way around. According to them, communication is a subset of marketing. In complete conformity with traditional marketing theory, communication is seen as something that does not enter the picture until the marketing plan and strategy have been worked out.[24] From this point of view, marketing is a discipline that belongs on the strategic level in the company, while communication is reduced to a supplementary discipline at operational level. Marketing works with all four of the Ps (product, price, place and promotion) while communication is limited to the promotion, or perhaps even just a part of promotion. One of the marketing people expressed her pleasure in her work like this: 'It is more fun to be the person that casts the cannon ball,' she said. 'I'm happy enough to let someone else load it into the cannon and fire it. Marketing is a much heavier and more time-consuming process than communication', she claimed. The communications people 'just put their hands out and are given lots of delicious ingredients, and then they go off and bake a lovely cake, or whatever.' Most of the marketing people shared this point of view and felt that marketing should be the client in relation to communications.

Communications and marketing are complementary

The vast majority of people in the new, integrated department felt that their own discipline or professional skills were located at a higher strategic level than that of the counterpart, and that their discipline should therefore assume a leading role in both the department and the organization as a whole. The interesting aspect of this view is that integration is seen as something that necessarily implies a hierarchical relationship between the different disciplines. An equal or parallel relationship is seen as an expression of disintegration and is expected to result in conflict between the disciplines. Very few employees perceived the relationship between the communications and marketing disciplines as non-hierarchical.

Veracity and objectivity versus manipulation and subjectivity

The decisive difference between communications and marketing, according to one of the communications-trained staff, is that communications is concerned with information, which he felt was more objective, while marketing is concerned with creating sales and is therefore more subjective. One of the staff from the old marketing department, but whose educational background lay mainly in communications, held a similar view of the difference between communications and marketing. She expressed it as a matter of manipulating reality, as opposed to being faithful to it:

> [In] marketing you consciously try to manipulate reality and force someone to do something. I mean, at bottom, marketing is about making people aware that they have needs, and that you can fill those needs if they buy something now and so on, whereas communication requires you to be more faithful to reality, and there are limits on how far you can twist and turn the truth.

A marketing colleague, trained in marketing, was in fundamental disagreement with her. He felt that the view of marketing as a manipulative and superficial discipline compared to communication expressed a lack of respect for the former.

THE ROLE OF TEACHING AND TRAINING

According to KMD's managing director, it is an expression of ignorance to claim, as many of the marketing people did, the discipline of marketing is located at a superior strategic level to communication, and that communication is not a discipline in itself, but merely one of the marketing disciplines. The source of this ignorance, according to the managing director, is the educational background of the marketing people:

> It's because they don't know any better, to put it crudely. They have been schooled through their places of education and the jobs they have had. So how would they know otherwise? There's nothing strange about that. I think anyone who has been

schooled in a particular direction will have a certain way of looking at things. And it's only natural that you hold onto the way you have been trained.

Not surprisingly, the marketing people felt that the managing director's view expressed a lack of respect for and knowledge about the marketing discipline in both theory and practice. The managing director's educational background was in journalism and in his previous career he had worked in PR and journalism, not marketing. One of the ordinary staff members, who had a professional background in communication, felt that there is a clear correlation between people's educational background and their view of reality. One of the factors contributing to creating this difference, in her opinion, is language. Since communication and marketing express themselves in different professional languages, they also possess different perspectives on reality:

Your education has a major effect on the way you see the world. You are greatly influenced in one way or another by your education and by the place you come from, whether it is a business school or a university, or technical training. So while I think it is more than just a language barrier, I also feel that a great deal is expressed in language, and that language helps to define your reality and creates slightly different worlds, whether this is a world full of purchasing centres and customers, or of stakeholders.

In this person's view, a factor of central importance was whether you viewed and described your surroundings through the concepts of customers or stakeholders. The difference between customers and stakeholders, according to this staff member, is that the former are people with whom you enter into an economic transaction (i.e. customers pay for a product that the company supplies). Stakeholders, on the other hand, are a much broader category, she says, as they also include potential staff members, partners, politicians, journalists and many others. Different linguistic practices, in her opinion, thereby result in different patterns of behaviour. You approach reality and the various players who inhabit it in different ways, depending on whether you view your surroundings on the basis of a market logic or a stakeholder logic.

THE QUEST FOR A COMMON UNDERSTANDING OF INTEGRATION AND A COMMON WORLD VIEW

At the introductory seminar in the new integrated department, a working group, entitled the Integration Group, was established. This group was given the task of operationalizing the concept of integrated communication and compiling material for a presentation of integrated communication in the company (e.g. on 'KMD info', the intranet for KMD staff) so that all the company's staff could learn more about what integrated communication involves, and the reasoning behind the integration of the communications and marketing departments. A member of staff from the old communications department remarked that it would have been a good idea to 'find a common language and culture' before commencing the work of goals definition (i.e.

the work of reaching the overall goals of the department and the company). The reason why this did not happen, according to this member of staff, was that the head of the department was very concerned with what other people thought, especially the other managers. For this reason he believed it was very important to first tackle the visible aspects such as the company's corporate design. The incentive structure in KMD is designed in such a way that the personal goals of the communications and marketing manager are closely associated with the goals of the department. It quickly became obvious to the members of the Integration Group that the marketing people and the communications people had problems 'understanding each other' and had very divergent views on exactly what integrated communication was. Consequently, some internal clarification work was initiated as the group felt that it was first necessary to agree on what the concept meant before telling the intraorganizational surroundings about integrated communication and the reasons why it had been introduced to KMD.

At a couple of meetings of the Integration Group, some mini-workshops were carried out on the semantic and conceptual aspects of the integration of the communications and marketing disciplines at KMD. The goal was to create a kind of 'dictionary' of the professional languages of the two disciplines, and to identify what staff saw as their similarities and differences. These sessions gave rise to some heated discussions, with some of the participants coming close to tears on at least one occasion. The idea of compiling a small 'dictionary' arose from the wish of the external researcher and consultant to discover which differences were in fact real, and which were merely due to technical complications and misunderstandings. The participants should first of all list all the functions, skills or tasks which were performed by marketing and communications, respectively. These points were then reviewed one by one to discover whether the activity in question was unique to the relevant discipline, or whether something similar, possibly going by another name, was also part of the portfolio of the other discipline. For both disciplines, the list exceeded 30 points. Of these, only a very few, according to the participants, were entirely unique to one of the disciplines. Tasks which were unique to marketing included sales support, sales management and product naming. Tasks which were unique to communications included such tasks as lobbying and press relations. The 'correctness' of the result of the dictionary exercise is naturally open to discussion, but the workshop achieved its desired aim: to initiate a discussion of the special characteristics of each discipline and the affinity of their work areas, as well as to assist in terminological clarification. The dictionary made it possible for the members of the group to understand languages and concepts of both disciplines, despite their professional differences. The differences between the communications and marketing people encompassed, however, more than just questions of terminology; their views of the surrounding world also diverged. The communications people saw KMD's surroundings as consisting of a wide range of stakeholders, including customers, users, politicians, partners, staff and potential new staff members, whereas the marketing people regarded only the customers as the target group, and 'when activities such as the above were carried out, it was only in order to reach the customers by an indirect channel'.

ESTABLISHING A COMMON VIEW OF INTEGRATION

The results of the work of trying to arrive at a common world view and under-standing of integration were presented at a unit meeting at KMD in Odense on 15 December 2004. Even a full year after the commencement of the work of the group, it was still not possible to present an entirely unanimous view of what integrated communication was about. The presentation therefore encompassed two different definitions of integrated communication: one compiled by group members with a professional background in communication, and the other compiled by a group member with a professional background in marketing. It was not until January 2005 that a single version was agreed. Unity on this question was achieved only when the marketing person who had most intensely defended what she saw as professional marketing interests in the conceptualization work went on maternity leave. The final definition of integrated communication was worded as follows:

> The task of integrated communication is to align and co-ordinate messages, external contact and development so as to ensure that the communications and marketing work comprises a coherent whole, and that customers and stakeholders are presented with a clear and consistent image of KMD. This is achieved via control of what we say, what we write, what we show, and what we do.

Integrated communication, the presentation went on to say, is not a discipline carried out by the communications and marketing department alone, but by the whole company. The implication of this statement is that the communications department should move from primarily communicating on behalf of the organization to assisting the organization to communicate more on its own behalf. In other words, a shift has occurred from the classic communications role towards the role of a communications facilitator.

THE END OF THE STORY

At the beginning of 2007, communications and marketing were separated once again. According to two staff members who were employed with the company at the time of the division, this was because the manager of the combined department was not strong enough – neither internally, in relation to the department itself, nor externally, in relation to the company's other management players. He regarded interest coali-tions and interest conflicts as a natural part of his work and a necessary prerequisite for the continued existence of the department, but he did not succeed in retaining power in relation to the other department managers. He therefore lost one-half of his acquired territory: marketing. Shortly after the break-up of the combined communi-cations and marketing department, he moved to a managerial position in another organization. Communications is now once again an independent department. The marketing department, just as before the amalgamation, is led by the head of sales, who now bears the title 'Sales and Marketing Director'.

In addition to professional and social skills, changes in companies are often influenced by power struggles between different areas and different people. As we have seen, this is also a decisive element in this case.

LESSONS LEARNED

This case study has taught us the following:

- The structures of the department and the company, and the organization of the work must support and provide opportunities for cross-work, and cooperation between the various professional areas.
- The level of knowledge of and familiarity with the work of 'the others' must be improved, so as to sweep away false prejudices.
- It may be of benefit to a company to undertake terminological and conceptual clarification in order to identify the genuine differences and similarities between the disciplines, and avoid unnecessary misunderstandings.
- The various players must respect each others' professional skills.
- Problems and challenges should be tackled in a zero-based manner, and not by each individual discipline separately, as this may lead to the problem or task being defined and solved on the basis of narrow professional interests.
- A manager who possesses a good familiarity with the various professional areas and disciplines is best suited to orchestrate integrated communication.
- Honesty and openness with regard to intentions, implementation and priorities in connection with integration will make the process easier.
- It is essential to have an understanding of cultural differences, different communities of practice and different ways of doing things.
- Integrated communication is not necessarily synonymous with univocality or unanimity, but it can encompass diversity, complementarity and plurality.

Appendix 11.1

The empirical part of the case study was conducted from December 2003 to January 2005. The case study was both type 'one holistic' and 'embedded holistic' (Yin 2003). In so far as the research concerned the integrated department as a whole, the first type came into play, while in so far as it focused on the department, as consisting of two parts (i.e. the two old departments whose staff had been socialized within the old structure and developed their professional identities accordingly). It might also be called an 'embedded holistic' study. In embedded holistic case studies the research is focused on a single field with embedded subfields or individuals, while in type one holistic single case studies dealing with a group the study may, for example, include all the members of that group and their mutual relationships (Maaløe 1996: 69–70).

In the study I used a participatory, open and direct technique in both structured and unstructured observation. All those employed in the department at the point of integration were interviewed. I was present at and/or participated in several working groups that had been entrusted with the task of working on the actual integration process or other areas especially vital to it.

The data comprised of:

- interviews with all the employees in the department at the point of integration, with some employees being interviewed twice;
  - 31 semi-structured interviews lasting 75–150 minutes.
- informal conversations;
- observation studies:
  - participation in unit meetings, group meetings and local department meetings;
  - participation in and attendance at workshops, seminars and courses, as well as simply being present in the department.
- email correspondence;
- diverse printed materials, such as annual accounts, reports, notices and minutes of meetings, working documents, brochures, etc.;
- presentations from internal meetings in the department and management meetings and presentations addressed to other parts of the company;
- the company's website;
- artefacts;
- author's own notes, photos and video sequences (made with a view to retaining impressions and atmosphere).

The interviews were transcribed in full and then coded. The interviews and coding were then transferred to ATLAS.ti 5. The coding was both inductive and deductive (Olsen 2002; Rasmussen and Østergaard 2002). More precisely, it was *in vivo* (Strauss

1987; Muhr and Friese 2004), which in this case means that it was carried out on the basis of certain key words and concepts that the interviewees themselves emphasized as being of key importance and characteristic of the integration project in the organization. The coding was also *in vitro*, meaning that I arrived at the codes with the help of the interviews, and sociologically constructed in the sense that the codes were constructed on the basis of concepts and theories derived from my reading of the research literature in the field (Strauss 1987). The codes were then grouped into so-called 'families' (i.e. themes that stood out in the coding process and in the subsequent review of all the codes as potential meaning-saturated conglomerates).

In May 2009 I undertook an extended telephone interview with two former employees of KMD with a view to finding out what had happened in the company with regard to the organization of and relations between PR and marketing since I concluded the original research project at the company.

NOTES

1 J. Cornelissen, *Corporate Communications: Theory and Practice*, London: Sage, 2004, p. 38.
2 Ibid.
3 L.T. Christensen, Firat, A.F. and Torp, S. 'The Organization of Integrated Communications: Toward Flexible Integration', *European Journal of Marketing*, 2008, Vol. 42 No. 3/4, pp. 423–452.
4 K. Hallahan, 'Toward a typology of organizational relationships between public relations and marketing', paper presented at Public Relations Division, Association for Education in Journalism and Mass Communication Conference, Montreal 1992.
5 Pickton, D. and Broderick, A. *Integrated Marketing Communications*, 2nd edn, Harlow, England: Prentice Hall, 2005.
6 M.M. Lauzen, 'Public relations roles, intraorganizational power, and encroachment', *Journal of Public Research,* 1992, Vol. 4–2, p. 69.
7 Hallahan, op.cit.
8 Hallahan, op.cit.
9 D.E. Schultz, D.E. and Kitchen, P.J., *Communicating globally. An integrated marketing approach*, Chicago: Palgrave, 2000, pp. 169–170.
10 E.g. T. Duncan, T. and Claywood, C. 'The Concept, Process, and Evolution of Integrated Marketing Communication', in E. Thorson and J. Moore (ed) *Integrated Communication: Synergy of Persuasive Voices*, Mahwah, New Jersey: Lawrence Erlbaum Associates, 1996, pp.13–34.
11 E.g. T. Yeshin, *Integrated Marketing Communications. The holistic approach*, Oxford: Butterworth-Heinemann, 2003; S.E. Moriarty, 'PR and IMC: The benefits of integration', *Public Relations Quarterly*, Vol. 39(3), 1994, pp. 38–44; Pickton and Broderick, op.cit.
12 K. Eiberg, 'Marketing public relations', in K. Eiberg, E. Karsholt and S. Torp (ed) *Integreret markedskommunikation*, Danmark: Samfundslitteratur, 2008, pp. 152–153.
13 T. Duncan, 'Integrated marketing? It's synergy', *Advertising Age*, March 8, 1993.
14 Schultz and Kitchen, op.cit.
15 A.L.M. Van den Bosch; De Jong, M.D.T. and Elving, W.J.L., 'How corporate visual identity supports reputation', *Corporate Communications: An International Journal*, Vol.10 No.2, 2005, pp. 108–116.
16 L.T. Christensen and Cheney, G., 'Self-Absorption and Self-Seduction in the Corporate Identity Game' In M. Schultz, M.J. Hatch and M. H. Larsen (eds) *The Expressive Organization*, Oxford: Oxford University Press, 2000, pp.246–270.
17 Christensen, Firat and Torp, op.cit.

18 L.E.G. Åberg, 'Theoretical Model and Praxis of Total Communications', *International Public Relations Review*, 13(2), 1990, pp. 13–16.
19 J. Kunde, *Corporate Religion. Building a Strong Company through Personality and Corporate Soul*, London: Prentice Hall, 2000.
20 L.T. Christensen, Morsing, M. and Cheney, G., *Corporate Communications. Convention, Complexity and Critique*, London: Sage, 2008.
21 E. Thorson and Moore, J. (ed) *Integrated Communication: Synergy of Persuasive Voices*, Mahwah, New Jersey: Lawrence Erlbaum Associates, 1996.
22 C. Fill, *Marketing Communications: engagement, strategies and practice*, 4th ed, Harlow, England: Prentice Hall, 2005, pp. 310–312.
23 S. Torp, 'Integrated Marketing Communication(s) or Integrated Communication(s)? When terminology matters', in K. Podnar and Z. Jancic (eds) *Corporate and Marketing Communications as a Strategic Resource; Response to Contempory use, Challenges and Criticism*, Ljubljana: Spon press. 2008, pp. 21–29.
24 E.g. J. Burnett and Moriarty, S., *Introduction to Marketing Communications. An Integrated Approach*, New Jersey: Prentice Hall, 1998.

REFERENCES

Åberg, L. E. G. (1990) 'Theoretical Model and Praxis of Total Communications', *International Public Relations Review*, 13(2), pp. 13–16.
Burnett, J. and Moriarty, S. (1998) *Introduction to Marketing Communications. An Integrated Approach*, New Jersey: Prentice Hall.
Christensen, L.T. and Cheney, G. (2000) 'Self-Absorption and Self-Seduction in the Corporate Identity Game' in M. Schultz, M.J. Hatch and M. H. Larsen (eds) *The Expressive Organization*, Oxford: Oxford University Press, pp.246–270.
Christensen, L.T., Firat, A.F. and Torp, S. (2008) 'The Organization of Integrated Communications: Toward Flexible Integration', *European Journal of Marketing*, 42(3/4), pp. 423–452.
Christensen, L.T., Morsing, M. and Cheney, G. (2008) *Corporate Communications. Convention, Complexity and Critique*, London: Sage.
Cornelissen, J. (2004) *Corporate Communications: Theory and Practice*, London: Sage.
Duncan, T. (1993) 'Integrated marketing? It's synergy', *Advertising Age*, March 8, p. 22.
Duncan, T. and Claywood, C. (1996) 'The Concept, Process, and Evolution of Integrated Marketing Communication' in E. Thorson and J. Moore (ed) *Integrated Communication: Synergy of Persuasive Voices*, Mahwah, New Jersey: Lawrence Erlbaum Associates, pp.13–34.
Duncan, T. and Moriarty, S.E. (1998) 'A Communication-Based Marketing Model for Managing Relationships', *Journal of Marketing* 62, April, pp. 1–13.
Eiberg, K. (2008) 'Marketing public relations' in K. Eiberg, E. Karsholt and S. Torp (ed) *Integreret markedskommunikation*, Denmark: Samfundslitteratur.
Fill, C. (2005) *Marketing Communications: engagement, strategies and practice*, 4th edn, Harlow: Prentice Hall.
Muhr, T. and Friese, S. (2004) *User's Manual for ATLAS.ti 5.0*, 2nd edn, Berlin: Scientific Software Development.
Glaser, B.G. and Strauss, A. (1967) *The Discovery of Grounded Theory: Strategies for qualitative research*, Chicago: Aldine.
Hallahan, K. (1992) 'Toward a typology of organizational relationships between public relations and marketing', paper presented at Public Relations Division, Association for Education in Journalism and Mass Communication Conference, Montreal.
Kunde, J. (2000) *Corporate Religion. Building a Strong Company through Personality and Corporate Soul*, London: Prentice Hall.
Lauzen, M.M. (1992) 'Public relations roles, intraorganizational power, and encroachment', *Journal of Public Research*, 4–2, pp. 61–80.

Moriarty, S.E. (1994) 'PR and IMC: The benefits of integration', *Public Relations Quarterly*, Vol. 39(3), pp. 38–44.

Maaløe, E. (1996) *Case-studier af og om mennesker i organisationer*, København: Akademisk Forlag.

Olsen, H. (2002) *Kvalitative kvaler. Kvalitative metoder og danske kvalitative interviewundersøgelsers kvalitet*, Denmark: Akademisk Forlag.

Pickton, D. and Broderick, A. (2005) *Integrated Marketing Communications*, 2nd edn, Harlow: Prentice Hall.

Rasmussen, E.S. and Østergaard, P. (2002) *Samfundsvidenskabelige metoder. En introduktion*, Gylling: Odense Universitetsforlag.

Schultz, D.E. and Kitchen, P.J. (2000) *Communicating globally. An integrated marketing approach*, Chicago: Palgrave.

Strauss, A. (1987) *Qualitative Analysis for Social Scientists*, Cambridge: Cambridge University Press.

Thorson, E. and Moore, J. (ed) (1996) *Integrated Communication: Synergy of Persuasive Voices*, Mahwah, New Jersey: Lawrence Erlbaum Associates.

Torp, S. (2008) 'Integrated Marketing Communication(s) or Integrated Communication(s)? When terminology matters', in K. Podnar and Z. Jancic (eds) *Corporate and Marketing Communications as a Strategic Resource; Response to Contempory use, Challenges and Criticism*, Ljubljana: Spon Press. pp. 21–29.

Van den Bosch, A. L. M., De Jong, M. D. T. and Elving, W. J. L. (2005) 'How corporate visual identity supports reputation', *Corporate Communications: An International Journal*, 10 (2), pp. 108–116.

Yeshin, T. (2003) *Integrated Marketing Communications. The Holistic Approach*, Oxford: Butterworth-Heinemann.

Yin, R.K. (2003) *Case Study Research. Design and Methods*, 3rd edn., Thousand Oaks, California: Sage.

12

Public relations model of a socially responsible company

Case study of Coca-Cola Beverages Hrvatska[*]

MAJDA TAFRA-VLAHOVIĆ

INTRODUCTION

Corporate social responsibility (CSR) is defined in different ways. According to one of the definitions, CSR refers to 'achieving commercial success in ways that honour ethical values and respect people, communities, and the natural environment' (*Business for Social Responsibility*). Bagic, Skrabalo and Narancic (2004, p. 15) offer a descriptive definition of CSR. It is about:

> a company assuming responsibility for its activities that go beyond commercial considerations. For some it is looked at as the source of competitive advantage; for others it is an important response to the increasing demands of key stake-holders, such as employees, investors, consumers and environmentalists.

We are witnessing extremely fast and dynamic development in this area of CSR, with almost exponential growth of investment in such activities. Indeed, the term 'CSR movement' is already in use. For many organizations, the aim of becoming a socially responsible company has become a business imperative.

This is also the case for Coca-Cola Beverages Hrvatska (CCBH) the company that produces and sells soft drinks of the brands owned by The Coca-Cola Company in Croatia. Today, the company is recognized as the leader in the context of CSR in Croatia and beyond, since in 2003 CCBH was the first company in the whole Coca-Cola system that had published a social report.

---

[*] current name Coca-Cola ABC Hrvatska, member of Coca-Cola Hellenic Group.

At the beginning of the new decade in 2000, however, CSR as a concept and a corporate policy had not received much attention within multinational companies. In Croatia, only a couple of companies, CCBH included, had previously published only their environmental reports.

The gradual implementation of CSR in the operations of Coca-Cola in Croatia, and the advocacy and promotion accompanying it, was, by no means a classical public relations campaign. The transformational change of Coca-Cola Beverages Hrvatska from a marginal player in the new emerging business policy of corporate social responsibility in Croatia to a leader was a strategic and operational direction led by the General Manager and the company's public relations function. This change gradually increased the positive reputation of the company, marking it out as a leader in terms of CSR development in Croatia and Central and Eastern Europe. The steady evolution of the company's CSR activities affected the initial model of public relations that had predominantly been used within the company as the process of embedding CSR had evolved. In fact, the change of public relations practice based on a monolithic one-way form of communication with various audiences through direct contacts or through media channels to an interactive stakeholder dialogue-based model was first fully publicly and internally recognized when Coca-Cola Beverages Hrvatska published its first social report based on the *Global Reporting Initiative Guidelines 2* in 2003. This positioning was further reinforced in 2005, when CCBH was again the first company in the country to have used the newly issued *Global Reporting Initiative Guidelines No 3* in its sustainability report in 2005. To comply with these guidelines meant that it was necessary for the company to undertake far more complex research, and greater transparency and accountability.

CONTEXTUAL RESEARCH

In 2000, therefore, CCBH and its public relations function had no particular benchmarks or examples of excellence within the Coca-Cola system to look to. This turned out to be positive because the Coca-Cola system had not imposed any restrictions or guidelines on the bottlers and was fully supportive of local initiatives.

The whole process was driven by General Manager Bruno Filipi and the Public Affairs and Communication Manager of CCBH (author of this text) who investigated and led the process. Empirical research in the area of public relations in the case of CCBH was thus a longitudinal study which had started before the company had first introduced the policy CSR. It continued for three years. Developing the empirical research involved examining theories and relevant secondary research that had been previously conducted. As a result, ten variables for empirical research were set up. Both qualitative and quantitative methods were used. In total, during three years, seven surveys on various convenient samples were conducted. Fifty in depth, semi-structured interviews and one focus group were held. In addition, there was a qualitative analysis of the written inputs provided by various participants.

The public relations manager had direct contact with the people involved and the situation on the ground. Moreover, the author's personal experience and insight were an important part of the research and necessary for understanding the phenomenon.

Because the situation both within and outside CCBH was dynamic, there was considerable caution regarding any call for change and indeed, about any assumption that change was necessary. Indeed because the public relations manager herself was both an observer and a participant in the company herself, she was caught up in the dynamics of the change process while also being an observer of the processes taking place.

GOALS AND OBJECTIVES

In the process of introducing and embedding CSR into the operations and policies of CCBH, the main goal was the creation of a synergistic value in three main areas:

1. increased reputation and legitimacy of Coca-Cola brands and The Coca-Cola Company and Coca-Cola Hellenic Company in Croatia and globally;
2. increased competitive advantage as a result of turning potential risks into corporate social opportunities;
3. increased quality of relationships with various stakeholders at local and national levels enriched by pro-active and interactive communication.

Over the course of five years (since 2000), at the initiative of the General Manager and the Public Relations function, CCBH developed and embedded the key principles of CSR in the business strategy of the company. This had, in return, significantly changed the company stakeholder communication from one-way public information and two-way asymmetrical communication to a more obvious two-way symmetrical stakeholder and public-focused communication.

COMMUNICATION STRATEGIES

A new insight advanced by Gregory and Tafra (2004, p. 65) regarding various stakeholder expectations in the context of corporate social responsibility in corporations defines them in terms of two variables. One is relationship intensity, the degree to which each must take into account the needs of the other. The further apart the parties are, the less need there is to accommodate the other's view in discussions, and the lower the level of engagement; the closer together they are, the more the dialogue is characterized by mutual accommodation, respect, understanding and consideration. The other is content expectation, meaning that content expectations of CSR programmes will vary according to the social and cultural context. These may be related to the immediate business environment. They are paramount in countries where democratic government is evolving or unstable, which was the case in Croatia.

Strategies used by the company in embedding CSR included, among other actions, media-based advocacy, with particular focus on the local media. Within the organization, strong social capital building and networking was initiated by the public relations department. It cascaded through the organization to the middle management level with targeted messages of responsible business and sustainable development.

Implementation of corporate social responsibility in Coca-Cola Beverages Hrvatska over a number of years generated profound changes in the functioning of the human resources (HR) department. HR introduced regular employee satisfaction and employee engagement surveys, following up with a set of actions immediately after having shared the results with the employees and including them in the search for solutions.

In the area of marketing, a cause-related marketing campaign was used at the beginning of the process. It targeted the city of Dubrovnik as it was the most attractive for the media and a number of stakeholders. It was followed by a number of similar national and local marketing strategies.

The company had also engaged in an increasing the number of environment-related projects, aiming to overcome the restrictions imposed on the company's operations by the law, which at the same time, contributed to the company being recognized as the CSR leader.

A great number of local community projects were launched. The majority of the projects were based on cross-sector partnerships and involved local authorities, which, somewhat to their own surprise, soon recognized Coca-Cola as a local partner and not some distant international player.

TARGET AUDIENCES

The scope of target audiences was very wide. For each element of the process it was based on separate stakeholder mapping and, in some cases, also related to risk assessment. On a more detailed level, different elements of the overall campaigns were targeted at specific stakeholder groups:

- consumers (cause-related marketing);
- journalists (media encounters and traditional media relations tools and strong networking);
- national government bodies (often not directly targeted by the company action but indirectly targeted through the local authorities with whom they had been in contact);
- local authorities (new established connections directly networked them with all global partners, including the company and the related global NGOs);
- employees (ongoing CSR-based internal communication and consultations processes);
- academia (directly involved in the reporting process);
- national and international NGOs (Prince of Wales International Business Leaders Forum endorsed the first report);
- caretakers in the field (teachers and NGO activists were directly involved in community projects).

This by no means exhausts the list of targeted audiences. However, one very positive outcome was a significant expansion and strengthening of the direct links and relationships that the company had established with targeted audiences it had never directly contacted before. The expansion in the number and type of stakeholder relationships posed new challenges for the public relations function of CCBH, demanding a new more symmetrical approach to stakeholder communications and interaction.

The public relations strategy involved a number of smaller campaigns which focused on the areas of market, workplace, community and environment. Two of these campaigns, however, have had a profound impact on the reputation of the company and on its positioning as a leader in CSR within companies in the region. They will be dealt here in more detail. One of them is a Dubrovnik project entitled 'Dubrovnik and Coca-Cola'; the other was a CSR reporting initiative which was unique in the whole Coca-Cola system at the time.

TWO CAMPAIGNS: BENCHMARKING CAUSE-RELATED MARKETING AND MAKING COKE HISTORY

The exhibition titled 'Dubrovnik and Coca-Cola, Unique and Everlasting' opened in April 2001 in the old historic centre of Dubrovnik on the Croatian coast. It marked a milestone in the implementation of the so-called CCBH's Dubrovnik project which unified the company's endeavours in the areas of sales and marketing and the areas of public affairs and communications. In cooperation with the city authorities local artists were invited to contribute their visions of the unique synergy of the brand of Coca-Cola and the brand of Dubrovnik. The visual deigns were exhibited publicly and the citizens invited to vote for the best solution. They were publicly stimulated to do so by the promise of Coca-Cola to match every vote with a kuna (local currency) to be donated for the maintenance of the valuable Duke's Palace in Dubrovnik, one of the town's biggest architectural treasures. Not only was this example of cause-related marketing best practice news for Coca-Cola presence on the Croatian market, but the exhibition itself was also a novelty for the citizens of Dubrovnik and Croatia who had not previously been acquainted with this type of corporate philanthropy. The event was greatly appreciated by citizens, policy makers and the media which stressed, in particular, the sensitivity with which Coca-Cola had approached the issue of designing a logo to be used locally in connection with the exhibition. The logo respected the unique beauty and value of the town's monuments of which its citizens are particularly proud.

The Coca-Cola and Dubrovnik project reached its climax in May 2001, when the exhibition closed and the best logo solution was identified. This campaign also resulted in a substantial increase in sales and increased positive local media coverage. The other parts of this project which also generated high profile in this tourist area packed with visitors during the season, fall into the category of community relations programs and the wider area of CSR. In other words, CCBH had been widely recognized in Dubrovnik as a good corporate citizen. Since the eyes of the whole country were most of the time directed at Dubrovnik, a lot of the company's general CSR record was generated from this source.

The company's social responsibility programme in Dubrovnik involved also some other projects, such as Coca-Cola environmental classrooms; a pre-school ecological kit designed by local teachers and tested in local kindergartens; The Breeding of Oysters, an ecological workshop involving students of Dubrovnik focusing on the value of water for a primary school; and regular cooperation with an art workshop Lazareti in hosting alternative art programs and various other national and international events for young people.

In June, the local media intensively covered the one-week cruise of the educational scientific ship *Nase More* (Our Sea) owned by the Ministry of Science. Following the co-operation between CCBH and Dubrovnik University, CCBH donated educational equipment to the ship. The university paid back CCBH by giving the company five days of cruising. The company then donated this cruise to the ecological groups of Dubrovnik primary and secondary schools. This co-operation of an educational and scientific institution with a company for the benefit of children from the local community was, at the time, a pioneering initiative in Croatia; the media and policy makers gave it a lot of attention.

The first social report was another milestone in embedding CSR policy and building a reputation. The fact that this was the first such report in the whole Coca-Cola system – in fact it was the first such report by a corporation in the region – was emphasized in an external review conducted by International Business Leaders Forum (IBLF) for Central and Eastern Europe. As Susan Simpson, the IBLF's then Director for Central and Eastern Europe stated in the introduction to the report, it was 'the first comprehensive social report to be produced at the country office level anywhere in the former Communist part of Europe' (*Coca-Cola Beverages Hrvatska: Social Report*, November 2003, p. 6). This initiative significantly contributed to the reputation of CCBH as a CSR leader and it also marked its place in the history of Coca-Cola. Indeed, as highlighted, this initiative represented

> the first social report, using an external consultant (Stubbs) and reporting according to the GRI guidelines, and was driven by a mixture of intellectual curiosity and clear leadership by a small group of senior managers. . . in the absence of any similar reports in Croatia and, indeed at that time, no reporting tradition within the parent company. In retrospect it was a 'brave' step involving considerable exposure, revealing the company's average annual salary and market share for the first time, and a degree of self-criticism (the results of an employee satisfaction survey were included explicitly for this reason). In the words of a senior manager, it involved 'opening ourselves up to our stakeholders and saying – well, this is what we are'. Turning a 'threat' into an opportunity, the report was a first step in terms of raising awareness within the company, and explicitly recognising the positive social impacts of aspects of the company's performance which had not, up to that point, been recognized; a kind of shift from a lack of recognition of competence to an increased awareness of competence.
>
> (Stubbs, Tafra and Redzepagic 2005, p.58)

RESULTS AND EVALUATION

Evaluation of the impact of the CSR embedment process was carried out using a combination of empirical research methods designed to gather responses from a range of internal and external stakeholders. Methods included in-depth interviews with regional managers within the company, public relations managers in 23 country operations belonging to the Coca-Cola HBC Group, journalists and partners. Surveys and observations of country public relations managers in 26 countries were also gathered, focus groups were held and content analysis of media coverage carried out.

The approach or model of public relations that lies behind the communication and establishment of the relationship of CCBH as a socially responsible company with its stakeholders since 2000 includes direct communication with interest groups and audiences on three levels: local, national and global. The approach to public relations observed in the case of CCBH can be seen to represent an essentially normative model of public relations practice in a socially responsible company, implying the need to develop and maintain effective dialogical relationships with all relevant stakeholder groups in what may often be a multi-stakeholder environment.

Moreover, a further lesson that emerges from this case is that effective stakeholder relationships cannot be assumed to be static. Rather, socially responsible organizations must recognize the need for a dynamic approach to developing effective dialogue with what may be a constantly changing set of stakeholders and stakeholder values, particularly when the organization in question is operating on an international scale or a global scale. Here it is important to recognize that stakeholders themselves will often engage in dialogue among themselves, building alliances and combining where interests coincide. Thus, in short, the potential network of relationships that any large socially responsible organization may need to attempt to manage can be highly complex and, moreover, in a state of constant flux.

For companies which operate as part of a large global corporation, such as CCBH, the socially responsible approach will rest on the global values of corporate citizenship, but it should also acknowledge the need to take account of local cultural specifics. A company that is a member of a global corporation cannot communicate effectively with different interest groups and audiences in the national environment by practising public relations unless it bases its strategy on the acknowledgement of specific local culture and interests. Thus, in the case of CCBH, its local communications and relationship-building strategies have been based on the local and regional socio-cultural values and patterns of behaviour found among the local community. In Croatia, the local quality of the strategy of a company such as CCBH, which is a part of a global corporation, does not only refer to its national focus (i.e. the balance between global and local determination), but it refers to its sub-national focus, regional focus and micro-local focus (on the region of Dalmatia and Dubrovnik for example.)

The example of CCBH suggests that if a company aspires to become an effective socially responsible company, CSR strategies should be effectively embedded in the business. This process should not only be fully supported by the leading coalition of the company but also fully initiated and orchestrated by the public relations function. Arguably, this process has four key elements. The first one is the stakeholder approach. This needs to be the dominating strategic approach in company's public relations. The overall power and influence of a stakeholder group is not only determined by its commercial or political strength, but by its social relevance and the general benefit it provides for society as well. In developing and maintaining a company's stakeholder relationship, the socially responsible organization remains sensitive and responsive to the interests of all its stakeholders and the application of the concept of social opportunity. The advantage of such an approach lies in the resulting quality of stakeholder relations, as well as the potential synergy and innovations in related business models.

The second element is two-way symmetrical communication. A certain number of the elements are directly tied to the concepts of social responsibility and business ethics. Those are above all the following: preference of a two-way symmetrical communication or the so-called 'mixed model' of communications management, which, in this case, could be said to imply a strategic role for public relations, transparency of operations and communication with audiences and stakeholders (i.e. a socially responsible approach to public relations).

The third element is public relations management as relationship building and the fourth element is recognising the cultural specificity of local identities. Such considerations are important in the first stage of a partnership project between the local community, private sector and civil society organizations particularly when the only source of project funding may be the private sector. In such cases, funds are often allocated in the form of the seed money necessary for the project to earn recognition of its benefit to the society so that regional or national authorities are then willing to pick up the project and raise it to the level of a regional or national program.

PUBLIC RELATIONS MODEL of Coca-Cola Beverages
Hrvatska as a socially responsible company

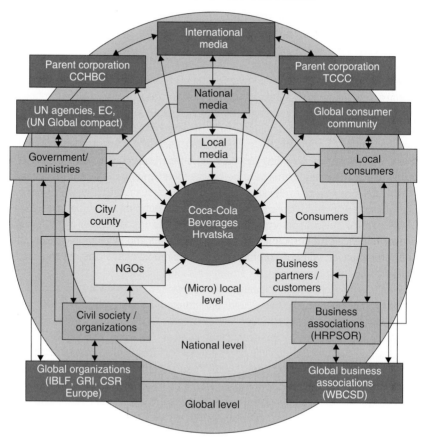

Figure 12.1 A normative model of public relations in a socially responsible company

As the model based on the example of Coca-Cola Beverages suggests, in a socially responsible company, public relations is significantly enriched by the partnership and various stakeholder communication channels that are likely to be developed by the company. Arguably the most important element of the model is the emphasis placed on the local level as a special level of partnership. This emphasis can help ensure that the public relations function and the company itself are closely attuned to local stakeholder interests and needs and that such considerations are carried through into communications and corporate policies adopted at the national level and, perhaps, international level.

This mediation of the local influence within national communication is a key characteristic of this model. The same mediation is also conducted on the global level, where a company communicates directly, but also indirectly, with global organizations. In fact, the direct relationships with certain groups on one of three levels (local, national, global) are also mediated by indirect relationships at the other two levels. This allows for total dialogue between all relevant stakeholder groups in a democratic atmosphere of open communication. This produces a type of communication that is responsible to all audiences.

CONCLUSIONS AND LESSONS

The introduction of the CSR policy can have a profound effect on the scope of the communications and public relations functions role and work of an organisation that moves to embrace the corporate social responsibility orientation.

The transition from a one-way communications model to a more dialogical basis for stakeholder communications often takes time, especially when such an orientation represents a total break from previous ways of operating.

For international companies, the process of developing a comprehensive CSR policy and supporting communications requires careful understanding of stakeholder interests and issues at the local, national and international levels.

Communications and public relations are of key relevance to social responsibility. The point of CSR lies in the overall *relations* with different social groups that might have an influence on a company or that could be influenced by a company. Business cannot be changed without communication; communication is the essence of its interrelation with the society.

The challenge in developing effective stakeholder communications lies in the numerous forms of communication that may exist between businesses and different audiences and stakeholders, some of them completely new and still undiscovered, in the framework of a social community as coalesced, interdependent, interactive, mutually effective, stimulating and interfaced segments. In short, public relations are a precondition and the essence of the transformation of business into responsible business.

Appendix 12.1

RESEARCH DESIGN: KEY RESEARCH QUESTIONS, HYPOTHESES AND METHODS

Research question	Hypothesis	Research area	Methods
RQ1 What are corporate social responsibility and public relations in Croatia like?	H1 CSR underdeveloped. Public relations undervalued in the society but on the rise.	NATIONAL ENVIRONMENT CROATIA	1. IN-DEPTH INTERVIEWS – PR MANAGERS 2. IN-DEPTH INTERVIEWS – JOURNALISTS OBSERVATION *TRIANGULATION – QUESTIONNAIRE SURVEY – TRAINING PARTICIPANTS – QUESTIONNAIRE SURVEY – PR MANAGERS – QUESTIONNAIRE SURVEY – BUSINESS HEADS*
RQ2 What is the corporate social responsibility strategy of the Coca-Cola Hellenic Bottling Company?	H2 Declaratively evolved. Awareness of CSR strengthened. Strategically positioned within businesses.	ORGANIZATIONAL ENVIRONMENT – Coca-Cola Hellenic Bottling Company	3. IN-DEPTH INTERVIEWS – CCHBC PR MANAGERS (23 COUNTRIES) 4. IN-DEPTH INTERVIEWS –MANAGERS IN THE REGION OBSERVATION *TRIANGULATION – QUESTIONNAIRE SURVEY – MANAGERS (26 COUNTRIES) – SELF-ASSESSMENT QUESTIONNAIRES – PR MANAGERS IN THE REGION – WRITTEN SUBMISSIONS – MANAGERS IN THE REGION*
RQ3 How is the corporate social responsibility of Coca-Cola Hellenic Bottling Company operationally implemented?	H3 Coordinated, operatively harmonized with other sectors, all-permeating.		
RQ4 What type of communication is used for communicating corporate social responsibility of Coca-Cola Hellenic Bottling Company?	H4 CSR communication of good quality, quality public relations.		

Research question	Hypothesis	Research area	Methods
RQ5 What was the public relations strategy of CCBH before the introduction of corporate social responsibility?	H5 One-way communication, public information model, no partnership.	FOCUS Coca-Cola Beverages Hrvatska	5. IN-DEPTH INTERVIEWS – LOCAL PARTNERS 6. FOCUS GROUP 7. QUALITATIVE CONTENT ANALYSIS OBSERVATION *TRIANGULATION*
RQ6 What is the public relations strategy of CCBH as a socially responsible company?	H6 Added value; internal cohesion; preference of micro-local cultural content.		*QUESTIONNAIRE* *SURVEY –* *EMPLOYEES, CCBH* *MANAGERS* *QUESTIONNAIRE* *SURVEY – THE* *PUBLIC ON CCBH*
RQ7 What is the public relations model of CCBH as a socially responsible company?	H7 Stakeholder dialogue. Two-way symmetrical communication. Stakeholder relationship nurturing. Specific directions of stakeholder communication – dialogue of all with all.		*REPORT* *(Abbreviations: CCBH –* *Coca-Cola Beverages* *Hrvatska; CCBHC-* *Coca-Cola Hellenic* *Bottling Company; CSR* *– Corporate Social* *Responsibility; 2WS –* *two-way symmetrical* *communication* *according to Grunig's* *fourth PR model; CC –* *corporate culture).*

REFERENCES

Bagić, A., Skrabalo, M. and Narancic, L., (2004), 'Overview of corporate social responsibility in Croatia' Academy of Educational Development, International Business Leaders Forum, Zagreb.

Coca-Cola Beverages Hrvatska: Social Report, November 2003, Coca-Cola Beverages Hrvatska, Zagreb.

Gregory, A. and Tafra, M., (2004), Corporate social responsibility: new context, new approaches and new applications; A comparative study of corporate social responsibility in a Croatian and a UK company, Proceedings of Bledcom, 2004

Stubbs, P., Tafra, M. and Redžepagic, D. (2005), Creating sustainability competences through reporting in Croatia, Enterprise in Transition, Split.

13

The Bolton brand

Place branding as an alternative approach to local authority corporate identity

RONNIE SEMLEY AND MELANIE POWELL

INTRODUCTION

Local authority corporate identity and its problems

All local authority PR practitioners are aware of the importance of a strong corporate identity to their council's communications strategy. However, anyone who has actually experienced the process of researching and implementing a new corporate identity for a local authority will be aware that achieving this can be fraught with difficulty. Within a council, political conflict, cultural differences and rivalry between departments, professional groups and geographically diverse offices can make it difficult to get the organization to think and act in a corporate manner, let alone agree upon a corporate identity and how to communicate it.

When a corporate identity process reaches the launch stage, many public sector communicators have faced the all too familiar sequence of the media criticism of costs which are perceived as being out of proportion to the benefits, political attacks from the authority's own councillors and widespread condemnation and resentment from local council tax payers.

The political dimension brings a number of additional challenges for the corporate identity planner. It may be hard to achieve the initial political will needed to address the need for a new brand, let alone fund its implementation. This issue also extends to that of perceived ownership; a new identity associated with an outgoing political administration runs the risk of being axed before its time to satisfy a political grudge instead of being axed for valid reasons.

In recent years, a number of local authorities have adopted an alternative approach. It is based on place branding rather than the traditional corporate identity model. Anholt defines an effective place brand as:

a plan for defining the most realistic, most competitive and most compelling strategic vision for the country, region or city . . . In all cases, it is fundamental to ensure that the vision of the place is supported, reinforced and enriched by every act of communication . . . The better strategies recognise that the principal resource of most places, as well as a primary determinant of their 'brand essence', is as much the people who live there as the things which are made and done in the place.

(Anholt 2003: 214)

At Bolton Council, the experience of using this more inclusive view of branding, backed by exploratory research (Semley 2007), suggests that this new approach can significantly reduce these problems and is much more effective in winning support from a wide range of stakeholders, who may become advocates and even champions of the new brand. This case study follows and reflects on the experiences of Bolton, a pioneer in this area. Bolton's early engagement with this approach enables useful conclusions to be drawn now.

BOLTON COUNCIL AND THE BOLTON BRAND

Bolton is a large metropolitan borough in the north of England. In early 2005, it began a process of consolidating its communications, marketing, PR, consultation and design staff into a single in-house Communications and Marketing Agency. This work was championed by the council's Director of Development and Regeneration and led by a newly-appointed Head of Communications and Marketing with strong brand awareness. Part of the role of the agency was to provide a home for the management of a planned new brand for the whole borough, not just the council. Since then, the new agency has facilitated the process of effectively planning and managing the new brand, both internally and externally.

From the outset, the council adopted a partnership approach, and looked substantially further than the organization itself in considering the question of local identity. The work was achieved in conjunction with many key partners, from both the private and public sector, and via 'Bolton Vision', the overarching name for the Local Strategic Partnership (LSP), to ensure buy-in at the right level and in the right context. As the largest employer in the borough, the council is the lead member of the LSP, but the important distinction of positioning the LSP, rather than the council, as the effective commissioner of the brand strategy was a key element of ensuring that the brand was seen as one for Bolton as a place, not just for the local authority. The LSP, therefore, initially led on the creation of the brand strategy, commissioning Manchester consultancy Hemisphere, which is experienced in similar public sector rebranding strategies, to work on its initial development.

A targeted consultation process in 2005 facilitated the creation of a brand that reflected the views of local residents and businesses, internal and external stake-holders and potential 'customers' of Bolton as a place (i.e. businesses and individuals who were potential investors, relocators or visitors). Once it was finalized, the council resolved to completely align itself with the brand, phasing out its existing identity in the process, and demonstrating its role as the leading LSP partner. The outcome was the stimulation of great interest in the borough in terms of general awareness and, more significantly, of continuing inward investment opportunities.

This is the story of the Bolton brand from its inception up to the present day, and the possible lessons for other local authorities which emerge from it.

WHOSE BRAND IS IT ANYWAY? AN OUTWARD-LOOKING APPROACH

Before the introduction of the Bolton brand, Bolton Council and its local partners had the same problem as many local authorities: over 60 different logos and messages which had grown up over time. As a result, messages were confused, with a detrimental effect on the town's ability to attract inward investment and visitors. Council services were not clearly badged as coming from the council, but from many different service points which residents would not necessarily have linked with their council tax payments.

For many local authorities in the past, corporate identity has been an inward-looking process. Arguably, the first important step towards the Bolton brand came in the way in which the council, along with its partners, considered the issue of branding. As an organiation firmly committed to tackling local issues with others through the LSP, the council envisaged the question of branding not as an internal organizational issue, but as an external place-related issue involving many different stakeholders.

This initial framing of the problem prompted the search not for a corporate identity for the council, but for a brand for Bolton itself, through the LSP. It also led to a multi-agency approach, bringing together the crucial elements of support from the then political leadership of the council, the chief executive and the council directorates alongside the partner organizations. External expertise and lessons learned from their experience of other local authority clients came from Hemisphere, with the newly-strengthened internal Communications and Marketing Agency acting as the home for the ownership, implementation and evaluation of the new brand, by agreement of all the LSP partners.

AUDIT AND RESEARCH: A WIDER CONSULTATION

In keeping with its outward-facing strategy, the council, in its role as lead member of the LSP, held detailed consultations with a range of local and regional stakeholders.

Tunnel vision about who shares in an organization's or area's identity and should therefore be included in initial research is often a weakness in corporate identity planning. This comes back to the communications planner in the form of stakeholders' resentment of the imposition of a brand which does not reflect their voices or aspirations. Whether for lack of time, resources or simply foresight, some organizations have historically excluded not only external audiences to the council such as local service users, but even large swathes of their own staff, who have been seen as unimportant because of lacking status or being based in outlying locations.

Other corporate identity processes which have engaged with local people who know the place well have then failed to balance this research with an investigation of perceptions, however under-informed, of the people they are aiming to influence – which in reality is the people who don't live in the area – (e.g. potential investors, relocators or visitors).

In contrast, ownership was the underlying theme of the aims of Bolton's consultation, which were:

- to understand and reflect the views of Bolton's internal and external customers – not just about what its key attributes were, but what its future opportunities and aspirations might be;
- to ensure that the outcome was meaningful and relevant to the people of Bolton, while at the same time being attractive and inviting to future developers, investors and tourists;
- to ensure that the work done was owned and endorsed by partners and stakeholders;
- to provide a good foundation of core brand values that would inform Bolton's behaviour as well as its promotion (i.e. to not just be a brand identity mark, but to be Bolton's visual representation).

As a result, Bolton's consultation in 2005 included council and partner staff, local residents, people who worked in Bolton, business and community leaders plus key partners and opinion formers from the wider region. It also sampled views from potential business investors and visitors from a number of key external locations to help understand the existing negative perceptions that Bolton as a place needed to counteract.

The consultation aimed to identify:

- respondents' current perception of Bolton;
- the key attributes which made up the real Bolton (i.e. the values and characteristics that distinguished it from other places);
- respondents' visions for the future (i.e. the challenges that people thought Bolton faced and the opportunities they thought were open to it).

The consultation also encouraged people to consider their emotional and aspirational responses to Bolton through a range of lateral value-association activities, such as drawing, mood-board association, colour selection and comparison of Bolton to other brands, such as makes or models of cars.

Hence the consultation extended further than the usual listing of key values, including wider local voices in identifying perceived challenges and opportunities and using the emotional responses to directly inform the look and feel of the final visual expression of the Bolton values. In doing so, the consultation empowered local people to make a more strategic and more creative contribution than a traditional corporate identity consultation process.

ANALYSIS, STRATEGY, PLANNING AND DEVELOPMENT

Consultation findings

The factual key themes about Bolton that arose from the consultation were:

- a strong sense of place and of history;
- a tradition of affluence;
- the affection people felt for it and its warmth and humour;
- a high level of inclusion and involvement in the community.

    The negative themes included:

- comfortable complacency with the status quo;
- untapped potential;
- a resistance to change and tendency to look backwards;
- difficulty in coping with the pace of change.

Bolton's brand values and essence

The emotional response findings of the consultation were distilled into a key set of values that people had identified as being recognizably Bolton. These were given a forward-looking slant to help inform behaviour and move Bolton away from some of the negative perceptions that had been identified:

- open: friendly, welcoming and inclusive;
- colourful: characterful, distinctive and interesting;
- sound: decent, reliable and trustworthy.

    Bolton's brand essence was also identified as

- 'family'.

    The underlying brand essence was identified as 'family', a word that captures the sense of belonging, involvement and affection that is so integral to Bolton's psyche.

What these meant for communication

In line with Anholt's observation that 'it is fundamental to ensure that the vision of the place is supported, reinforced and enriched by every act of communication' (2004: 214), each of the values was taken a step further to guide all communications about Bolton:

- open: being accessible, welcoming and relevant to the audience in content and appearance (i.e. 'I know what's in it for me');

- colourful: injecting the Bolton personality and character into all communications, using real people and local humour where appropriate for a down-to-earth local tone of voice even in official communications;
- sound: conveying decency, reliability and trustworthiness, communications should be down to earth, straightforward and direct (i.e. no flannel or hyperbole).

This last point is particularly important for council communications. Local authority communications often have to convey complex and difficult issues, deal with areas of risk and convey bad news. Through encouraging local people to talk about the negatives during the consultation, the council found that people do care about Bolton, despite a robust sense of its faults, and that this unconditional affection would endure such problems. By embracing Bolton's chosen themes of straight talking and the importance of sound, traditional values, Bolton's brand essence of family led it to a tone of voice which enabled these issues to be discussed in a familial way, telling it as it is and with a clear sense of differing opinions, but with underlying warmth and trust.

Creative exploration: design

Only once the values and essence had been agreed did Hemisphere move on to looking at their visual representation. This ensured that stakeholders were clear that the design of the visual identity, which is the part that most negative media coverage focuses on, was based on their views and feelings about the place. Hemisphere identified that a distinctive aspect of the consultation response was the very varied response people had to the colour exercise. This unusual variation was plotted graphically to try and get a sense of its meaning.

This translated into a vibrant mix of narrow stripes with wider ones representing the more popular colours. These inspired the new visual representation of the brand, which was subsequently christened 'Bolton's DNA'. The stripes were combined with a modified typeface, Bolton Clarendon. The typeface was chosen for its solid and down-to-earth characteristics, as well as a degree of quirk that reflected Bolton's sense of character. Together they form the core brand mark. The word 'Bolton' is typeset and filled with the DNA colour spectrum. There is even a subtle elephant's trunk device to the 't' in the word 'Bolton'. The device is a nod to the town's humour and reflective of the presence of elephants in a number of key Bolton symbols, including the town's coat of arms.

Figure 13.1 Bolton's core brand mark

The development of the core brand mark was crucial for several reasons:

- The word 'Bolton' was direct, straightforward and very flexible when applied to sub-brands.
- It embodied the spirit of the place brand ethos. Council staff, for example, now wear badges with the core brand mark rather than 'Bolton Council'.
- Its encapsulation of the distinctive Bolton DNA colour stripes made it virtually impossible to copy.
- The Bolton DNA within the branding was a constant visual reminder that the brand had come from the views of local people, and was not just thrust upon them.

Refinement and implementation

Second-wave consultation

Unusually, the implementation process started with a key additional step: a second consultation specifically to inform the process of implementation, communication and management. Drawing on the experiences of other local authorities in finding a traditional corporate identity process under attack by their own councillors and in local news media, these two groups were two of the key target audiences at this stage of the development.

This second wave of consultation set out to identify and address any concerns that might be raised about the new Bolton brand. It identified that the key issues were the perceived expense of the change and an incomplete understanding of how a new brand identity could help local organizations meet their goals more efficiently and benefit local people.

Each political party group was given its own briefing about the newly developed brand to ensure they were clear about the long-term benefits and short-term savings. Local news media were also briefed to ensure they appreciated the benefits of the change in terms of future savings versus initial outlay and understood the longer-term vision and benefits of the borough having its own distinctive identity.

As a result of this additional stage, councillors were highly supportive and initial local media coverage of the new brand was nearly 100 per cent positive. With these key opinion leaders largely buying in to the new brand, there was virtually no public or political backlash in the aftermath of the launch.

To further embed the value of the brand, once it had been in use for a few months, a short briefing document was produced to share with these and other key audiences. This two-page document clearly spelled out the cost of brand development, gave examples of the savings and efficiencies already identified as enabled by the new brand (which demonstrably outweighed the start up cost), listed prestigious early adopters of the mark and showed the benefits which were already accruing to the local area as a result of its adoption.

Implementation: Bolton Council

Implementation of the new brand within Bolton Council was gradual; it was included as items were replaced and updated. Advantages of using the new branding were clearly communicated to staff as:

- one council, stronger voice – clear, consistent communications to help to drive positive perceptions of the organization;
- efficiency – a unified approach to cut duplication of effort and save money;
- quality – a benchmark to improve and control the quality of communications;
- pride – a sense of pulling in the same direction, reflected through a strong and successful brand, making ambassadors of all staff;
- credit – consistently promoting services and maximizing the credit the council gets for the services it delivers.

While the ethos of the brand as applied in day-to-day communications and marketing ensured Bolton Council was always the hero and got the credit it deserved, the way in which the brand was applied to individual council services continued the inclusive approach which had been taken to the original research and design stages.

For example, to apply the brand to the promotion of specific functions of the Children's Services Department, the Communications and Marketing Agency enlisted the help of children and young people to find out how they felt their age groups should be represented through design using the new branding. The result was a series of silhouettes using the Bolton DNA stripes and representing age groups from a few months old to primary school age, up to age 11, young teens, older cool teens and young adults of 19. These designs were then used in many contexts, including in publications, on buildings and on vehicles used by Children's Services for these particular age groups. At the same time, the silhouettes also neatly sidestepped the tricky issue of ensuring fair and equal representation of the town's diverse communities in the council's marketing imagery.

A similar approach, including service users in the design process, was used for the process of applying the brand within many of the council's services.

Figure 13.2 Branded silhouette design used to promote Children's Services

Implementation: partner organizations

Outside the council, take-up and implementation of the brand was on a voluntary basis. The first organizations to adopt it were partners in the LSP. Early adopters included Bolton Wanderers Football Club, the Bolton Primary Care Trust, The Octagon Theatre, Bolton Fairtrade Foundation, Bolton CVS, the Safer Bolton Partnership, Emerson and Bolton School. All these partners retained their own branding, but with the addition of a specially-created partnership endorsement mark. This mark stated that they were part of the Bolton family in the highly recognizable graphic form of the core Bolton brand mark. Many other public and private sector organizations in Bolton have since adopted the brand, adding up to an unprecedented level of brand unity for a local area.

MONITORING, MANAGING AND MARKETING THE IMAGE

Evaluation

Early indicators of the effect of the brand included:

* anecdotal evidence from local businesses citing high awareness in the private sector, especially among developers;
* citation as an example of national best practice at the Regeneration and Renewal National Conference in 2007 and 2008;
* other local authorities citing Bolton's brand strategy as an example of good practice and asking for further details of the strategy and implementation plan;
* several award nominations and wins, including beating national campaigns for Scotland and Wales to win Best Corporate Identity in the National Roses Design Awards 2006.

There was intent to carry out a full comparative consultation in late 2007 to assess the effectiveness of the brand 18 months after its inception, but budgetary constraints precluded this. Instead, a more focused consultation took place for the Council's Development and Regeneration Department in 2008 into the effectiveness of the brand from a business and inward investment perspective.

This study repeated part of the original 2005 brand study by Hemisphere. Similar questions enabled comparisons to be made. Questions around brand recognition were also added. Telephone interviews took place with 29 key opinion formers. Respondents came from a broad cross-section of professional fields, including local and national governments, education, sport, the arts, creative industries, the media and key developers.

In the intervening three years a huge amount of work had been done to further the improvement and enhancement of Bolton by the council's Development and Regeneration Department, which worked with other council departments and the council's partners. This improvement and enhancement included:

- a new parking strategy;
- initial steps to encourage a café society;
- improvement of the town's retail offer (e.g. redeveloping the Market Place shopping centre);
- securing developer interest in Bolton via major developer forums;
- improving leisure facilities, including a new town centre pool;
- a strategy for the regeneration of Bolton's mills.

All this work was underpinned by integrated marketing and communication campaigns and materials using the Bolton brand.

In summary, in response to the questions asked of respondents:

- Two-thirds felt that the brand had made a positive and significant difference.
- The majority felt the brand was credible, saying it stands out from the crowd and reflects Bolton's originality, ambition and style.
- Over half associated themselves with the brand.

There was also a shift in the collated responses to the key themes and issues in relation to Bolton.

Key themes in 2005 included:

- a strong sense of place and of history;
- a tradition of affluence;
- the affection people felt for it, its warmth and humour;
- a high level of inclusion and involvement in the community.

Key themes in 2008 included:

- development and vision;
- approach to partnership working;
- ambitions for the future;
- positive, high-profile celebrities;
- strong industrial heritage.

Key issues in 2005 included:

- comfortable complacency with the status quo;
- untapped potential;
- resistance to change and tendency to look backwards;
- difficulty in coping with the pace of change.

Key issues in 2008 included:

- further improvements to Bolton town centre;
- frustration that the national identity still driven by northern stereotypes;
- a need to raise some residents' aspirations.

These changes reflect the work done by the council and its partners to shift perceptions, using the brand as a key lever to do this. In the key themes, history is still important, but there is now an acknowledgement of Bolton's ambitions. The town is now seen as looking to the future, while still acknowledging its illustrious past. Significantly, partnership working now comes to the fore.

The issues highlighted in 2005 all combined to create a sense of a reluctance to change in the town. In the 2008 findings, there is an acknowledgement of plenty more to do, but there is now a sense that the town is moving forward and a desire to ensure that residents share in the town's plans for future prosperity.

UPDATE

The qualitative consultation exercise in 2008 demonstrates that the brand has played a key role in shifting perceptions in and of the town.

The work undertaken since its launch has ensured that it has become a natural and instinctive process for the council and its partners to use the brand people want to be associated with its success. Given the acknowledged difficulties in keeping controlling of brands and corporate identities, particularly in large public sector organizations, this is a significant achievement in itself.

However, the Agency and its partners continue to evolve the brand through a strong branding approach across all key stakeholder groups. Some recent examples:

- destination events such as One Bolton, which is a two-month summer multicultural celebration and the annual Bolton Food and Drink Festival;
- development hoardings which encourage a sense of anticipation about what's to come;
- branded signage at all access points across the borough;
- integrated campaigns involving many partners, such as the local Be Safe Partnership's 'Operation Sherry' campaign, which encourage safe and sensible drinking;
- development of Bolton Life, a comprehensive 'what's on' website, which covers the events, festivals and culture of the town and complements an existing quarterly events brochure.

Bolton's approach to place branding has also resulted in huge interest from many other councils that are keen to learn from the success of the Bolton brand. The Agency has hosted many visits from these councils to share the benefits and lessons learned from their experiences.

KEY LESSONS LEARNED

Bolton's place branding approach has been effective and has succeeded in avoiding the major strategic issues which other local authorities have encountered in implementing corporate identity change in particular those relating to gaining support from staff at different levels and in different departments, local partners, local people, local news media and, crucially, elected members. What factors might have contributed to this, especially at a time when many local authority rebranding exercises fail or attract significant criticism? From their perspective Hemisphere, the agency initially responsible for the development of the brand, observed the following three key factors:

- Leadership: The championing of the brand process internally at an early stage by a senior non-marketing figure within the authority positioned the process as a fundamental part of Bolton's redevelopment and regeneration, not just a communications issue. The primary question was therefore 'What does Bolton want to be?', not just 'How should we promote it?'. The determined direction of the agency's work on the brand from day one by the Head (now Assistant Director) of Communications and Marketing was also crucial.
- Ownership: Brand implementation coinciding with the establishment of the Council's new Communications and Marketing Agency, meant that there was clear central ownership and a centralized management process. In other authorities where this is not in place it is extremely difficult to keep control of a new brand. Without strong control it is simply not as effective in changing perceptions and the value of the investment can be rapidly lost, adding to the view that branding is a waste of money.
- Discipline: The strong hand kept on the brand by the agency as a whole, often in the face of great internal pressures, has also been key to its effectiveness. In typical Bolton fashion, the agency was humorously nicknamed 'the Talibrand', but it is undoubtedly this tenacity, underpinned by the strong foundations of the brand's values and essence, which have made the Bolton brand a success.

Advantages of a place branding approach to corporate identity for the public sector include:

- Place branding has its roots in economic development. As such, it is aimed at improving the prosperity of the local area – an agenda which is non-political and capable of being endorsed by all local groups concerned with the area's future. In contrast, traditional corporate identity management for local authorities is vulnerable to being misrepresented as self-aggrandisement by a single, politically controlled organization using public money.
- Place branding looks wider than a single, politically controlled organization for its focus. It therefore offers a means of sidestepping the political difficulties which can face the corporate identify process for local authorities by offering collective ownership of a place brand which belongs equally to all partners involved in developing strategy for a local area, as well as to the people who make the area what it is.
- Since ownership of the brand is placed higher and wider than the council itself, it is less vulnerable to both political and interdepartmental conflict within the council. Rather than being seen as the property of one particular faction within the council, it is clearly a well-substantiated representation of the wishes of a broad range of local stakeholders, therefore it is less vulnerable to attack.

- Place branding sits naturally with a local partnership approach, mirroring both current central government policy and likely future direction for local service provision. The natural home for place branding in this context is within LSPs. As these involve a range of organizations, not all of which have a political dimension, this will dilute the impact of party politics on the brand. This means that the resulting brand identity is less vulnerable to political agendas.
- The focus on place rather than organization also has important consequences for public involvement. People who are uninterested in or even resentful of their local council tend to have a genuine identification with their hometown and an interest in its future. They are therefore more likely to want to be involved in contributing to its brand through participation in consultations and to feel interest in and ownership of the local brand which results.

Specific lessons from Bolton's management approach to place branding include:

- The power of a second, specific consultation to inform the implementation stage: by anticipating a negative backlash from key opinion leaders and undertaking a second wave of consultation to achieve buy in from these groups, Bolton arguably avoided the conflict and criticism which has derailed, or at least damaged, many council identity programmes at this stage. Other local authorities can learn from both this approach and its timing in the process. The positioning of this stage of consultation after the research, strategy and creative development stages meant that there was already a concrete proposal for the identity to form the basis of discussion, as well as early examples of its cost effectiveness and impact on achieving key local priorities.
- Wide involvement combined with tight management accountability: a major strength of the place branding approach is its wide view of development and ownership of the brand. A potential corresponding weakness is the risk of diffusion of responsibility for management of the resulting brand. Bolton's experience to date indicates the need for the management of the place branding process to be handled by a strong and professional communications, marketing and consultation function within one of the partners and driven by a manager positioned as part of the dominant coalition within that organization. Hence Bolton's approach clearly combined a wide, inclusive approach to brand development with tight accountability for brand management, with ongoing management and monitoring clearly situated within the newly-formed Communications and Marketing Agency of Bolton Council, the major partner.

Place branding appears to offer local authorities a strong and inclusive approach to corporate identity which sits well with partnership approaches and is capable of circumventing many of the problems which affect traditional corporate identity approaches for the public sector. The number of local authorities using this approach is now increasing. Bolton's early experiences offer a hopeful example to public relations practitioners who want a fresh view of the question of the nature and ownership of the brand identity of local organizations and services.

REFERENCES

Anholt, S. (2003) 'Branding places and nations' in R. Clifton and J. Simmons (eds) *Brands and Branding*, The Economist/Profile Books, pp.213–226.

Semley, R. (2007) Place branding and corporate identity in the public sector: Challenges, opportunities and the 'Big Bang', Manchester Metropolitan University, Unpublished CIPR Diploma Project.

14

Chimney Pot Park

When a sales launch event became the news!

LISA ASHURST

INTRODUCTION

Chimney Pot Park is an urban regeneration project in Salford, England. It involved the radical transformation of 349 traditional Victorian terraced houses into modern new homes. The project was delivered by award-winning property developer Urban Splash, who started the building work for the scheme in 2005 and completed it in spring 2009.

This case study deals with the public relations campaign carried out by Urban Splash in the lead up to the first public sales launch of 108 houses in the development. These houses were bought by people off-plan over a year before they would be habitable. The sales launch was on Saturday, 8 April 2006. All 108 houses were sold in just two and a half hours.

BACKGROUND AND CONTEXT

Property developer Urban Splash was set up in Manchester, England in 1993 by Tom Bloxham MBE and Jonathan Falkingham. The company has an established reputation as a pioneer in urban regeneration and an advocate of modern design.

From a standing start and financed entirely through the reinvestment of profits, the company has created over 3,000 new jobs, 1,000 new homes and 500,000 square feet of commercial space.

Urban Splash has regeneration projects across the UK. These projects include: Castlefield, Manchester; New Islington, the third Millennium Community at east Manchester; Altrincham, Cheshire; Ropewalks, Liverpool City Centre; Royal William Yard, Plymouth; Fort Dunlop, Birmingham; Lister Mills, Lake Shore, Bristol, Bradford; and Midland Hotel, Morecambe.

The company has received over 280 awards to date for its commitment to architecture, design, regeneration and enterprise. Its award winning projects include: Timber Wharf, Box Works and Moho, Castlefield, Manchester; Vanilla Factory and Matchworks, Liverpool; and Silk Warehouse, Lister Mills, Bradford and Rotunda, Birmingham. Urban Splash has received 34 prestigious RIBA Awards for Architecture – the most ever received by a private property developer.

For more information about Urban Splash and its developments visit www.urban splash.co.uk.

During the period 2002 – 2005 Urban Splash held several very successful sale launch events for its developments across the UK. In October 2005 the company launched apartments for sale in Birmingham's iconic Rotunda building, which is located at the heart of the Bullring shopping centre in the city. Rotunda had previously been an office building but Urban Splash took the decision to turn it into 232 apartments creating the most sought after city centre address in Birmingham.

Until Chimney Pot Park, Rotunda was the most successful Urban Splash sales launch so far. Following a previous sales release to loyalty clients and investors, the company had 48 apartments remaining for sale and they were all sold in just three hours.

MORE ABOUT CHIMNEY POT PARK

The Langworthy area of Salford was once a highly populated, close-knit community. Unfortunately, in the 1980s and 1990s, the area suffered marked economic and social

Figure 14.1 Rotunda

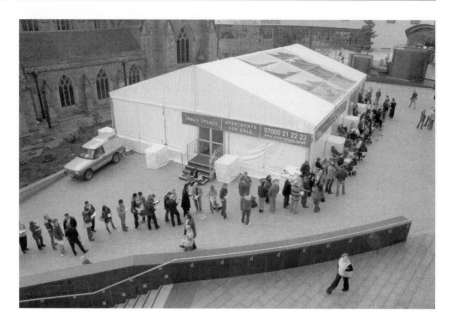

Figure 14.2 Rotunda launch

decline. It became associated with high levels of crime and social deprivation, seeing a lot of people leave the area. This left many houses, and in some cases whole streets, empty. Salford City Council decided something needed to be done to help regenerate the area.

Salford City Council acquired the site that is now Chimney Pot Park and all the houses on it. Their initial plan was to demolish all the traditional Victorian terraced houses and replace them with new, much more modern homes. They invited Urban Splash to look at the houses. With the company's background in working with old, sometimes derelict Victorian mills and warehouses, Urban Splash saw the potential to keep the best of the features of the houses but update them for the twenty-first century.

Working with Liverpool-based architects shedkm, the new design saw Urban Splash turn the traditional terraced house literally upside down.

Each house has two bedrooms on the ground floor, with the main living spaces located on the first floor. People who bought the houses could choose between having their kitchen or lounge on a new mezzanine level, which slots into the roof space.

Urban Splash retained the fronts of the houses and the streets, which are so familiar to viewers of the longest-running UK television soap opera *Coronation Street* which is set in a working class area of Salford (see http://www.itv.com/Soaps/coronationstreet/). However, in the new development at the rear of the houses the back alleyways are gone. Instead, a balcony, leading onto a terrace has been created at the first-floor level.

Underneath the new terrace, Urban Splash provided secure car parking and some street parking.

Figure 14.3 Before photograph of Chimney Pot Park

Figure 14.4 Before photograph of Chimney Pot Park

Figure 14.5 Computer-generated image (CGI) of plan

Chimney Pot Park was a partnership between Urban Splash, Salford City Council and national regeneration agency English Partnerships (now known as the Homes and Communities Agency). It forms one of several projects in Salford and Manchester that are part of the government's Housing Market Renewal and Pathfinder Areas.

Figure 14.6 Completed

Figure 14.7 Completed

The project itself has won the following awards:

- LABC Building Excellence Awards – Best Technical Innovation;
- What House? Awards 2008 – Best Affordable Development – Gold;
- Housing Design Award (DCLG, NHBC, RTPI, RIBA) 2008 – Overall Completed;
- *Mail on Sunday* Home Design Awards 2008 – Best Development;
- Concept for Living Design Awards 2008 – Best Use of Directional Design;
- RIBA Northwest Award for Architecture 2008;
- MIPIM Awards 2008 – Residential Development;
- *Grand Designs Magazine* Awards 2007 – Best Housing Project;
- MIPIM Architectural Review Future Projects Awards 2006 – Residential – Highly Commended;
- Housing Design Award (ODPM, NHBC, RTPI, RIBA) 2005.

For more details on Chimney Pot Park, see www.urbansplash.co.uk/chimney potpark.

THE PUBLIC RELATIONS CAMPAIGN

Objective

Following the success of Rotunda, when the time came to launch Chimney Pot Park houses for sale to the public, Urban Splash chairman Tom Bloxham set his sales, marketing and communications team a clear objective – to sell out the first phase of houses at the public sales for Chimney Pot Park. He recognised that there was already a strong buzz about the scheme and the marketing and communications team wanted to ensure everyone in the city would be talking about the scheme.

The first sales release was 108 houses. More than double the amount of properties sold at the Rotunda sales launch.

Planning and research

The unique design of the houses attracted positive press coverage since they were unveiled in 2003; periodically the image would crop up in a national newspaper heralding the design as the future of terraced housing.

The initial press coverage was positive and extensive, including a double-page editorial in the *Sunday Times* 'Home' section in late 2003. However, until the plans were approved, the public sector funding signed off and a development agreement between the partners signed, Urban Splash really did not want too much attention on the project. The reason for this is because it is important to generate demand at the right time (i.e. close to the sales launch) to convert as much interest into sales as possible.

At the end of 2005, Urban Splash was ready to begin the project. Urban Splash started on the site at the beginning of December 2005. It was decided to launch the houses for sale in spring: Saturday, 8 April 2006 was agreed.

Tactical campaign

Within a short time frame (beginning in January 2006), Urban Splash implemented a planned public relations campaign that was fully integrated with its marketing:

- The launch date was initially announced to a 15,000-strong Urban Splash database via the monthly email newsletter on 3 January 2006. www.chimneypotpark.co.uk also went live.
- The scheme was featured on BBC 1's *National Breakfast* news special on 6 January 2006. It featured an interview with Nathan Cornish, director of Urban Splash. The sales team received approximately 200 calls that day alone! The project was featured on BBC 2's *Culture Show* on 26 January 2006. Television coverage was arranged through established relationships with journalists and reporters at the BBC national news network and the producers of BBC 2 *Culture Show*.

Here is an example of press on Chimney Pot Park in the lead up to the launch from the *Sunday Mirror*.

Goodness knows what Jack and Vera would make of it, but the most famous back to backs in Britain are about to get a serious 21st Century makeover.

Five years ago, nobody wanted to live in the Langworthy area of Salford. Its back to back homes were hit by negative equity, rising damp and high local crime rates.

Now an ambitious £30 million redevelopment project called Chimney Pot Park will see these traditional homes revamped for new owners – and the regeneration is being seen as a possible blueprint of how to save other homes threatened with demolition.

Instead of knocking everything down and starting again, the facades of these familiar streets will be saved and large open plan, loft-style living rooms will be created upstairs with gallery kitchens, exposed roof beams and first-floor balconies with generous garden decking over secure car parking spaces below.

Karen Rockett

By the end of the first month, it was clear there was strong demand for the homes. The team decided to take a gamble and take the whole concept of the sales launch event to a new level.

Urban Splash decided to set up a temporary sales presence in Langworthy Park from Monday, 3 April 2006. From the Thursday night onwards, Urban Splash decided to invest in a M*A*S*H tent to allow people to camp out. The M*A*S*H tent was a large army-style tent which Urban Splash filled with camp beds for people to sleep on. It is a very unusual thing to do, but it is not very usual that people camp out to buy a house. All press releases and launch invitations plugged the M*A*S*H tent. To everyone's surprise and delight enthusiastic home buyers actually started to queue on Wednesday night!

Urban Splash also offered a number of houses to people living in the area immediately surrounding the scheme. This really started the press build-up to the sales launch. A press release was issued announcing the local sales launch and this was followed up with positive coverage in the *Manchester Evening News*.

Figure 14.8 M*A*S*H tent

Creative input

The M*A*S*H tent proved to be an inspired idea and many people who camped out said there was a real festival vibe; one woman said it was like being at the Glastonbury Festival. Perhaps the most pleasing result was that people actually got to know their new neighbours, over a year before they would be living in the houses. Many of the people who queued up remained in touch with each other and are neighbours today!

On 15 March 2006 Manchester's new radio station, Xfm, was launched on air. In the ten days leading up to broadcast, Chimney Pot Park was the online sponsor of the station's competition to choose the first song to be played. Urban Splash received 300 enquiries directly from the Xfm website.

Xfm was the station of choice for campers at the sales launch. Many of the campers had songs played throughout the launch day.

Results

Urban Splash continue to be the envy of many other developers because of their marketing ability. Boss Tom Bloxham reports that they have had serious inquiries from 900 people for their upside down houses in Langworthy, Salford now quaintly renamed Chimney Pot Park.

Jill Burdett

By Monday, 3 April 2006 the figure was 3,000. On Saturday 8 April Urban Splash sold 108 houses in two and half hours. People started to queue for their chance to buy from early Wednesday morning, camping out in April showers in Langworthy Park, over looking the site.

The success of the sales launch of Chimney Pot Park has become a clear example of what can be achieved when the private sector works in partnership with the public sector, in this case Salford City Council and English Partnerships.

A few highlights of the campaign include:

- 12 local people bought houses in advance of the public sales launch.
- 108 houses sold to the public in two and half hours on Saturday, 8 April 2006.
- Coverage for the launch was achieved in the *Mail*, *Guardian*, *Telegraph* and *Express*.
- There was a four-minute piece on BBC Radio 4 *Today* at 7.40am Thursday, 6 April 2006. It was followed by a phone call of congratulations from then Deputy Prime Minister Right Honourable John Prescott MP to Urban Splash's chairman, Tom Bloxham!
- There was coverage on BBC 1's national lunch time news on the Thursday before the launch.
- There was coverage on local TV both (BBC and commercial).
- A brand new community was in place before the houses were ready.
- There was a change in the perception of the area. It went from being perceived as a place where no one wanted to live to having a thriving new community with a real buzz about it.

Figure 14.9 Queue

- The press coverage reached an audience of over 18 million with an advertising equivalent value of £358,093.

The public relations and marketing campaign won the following awards:

- CIPR Pride Awards 2006/2007 Presidents Grand Prix – In-house Campaign;
- CIPR North West Pride Awards 2006 – In-house Campaign – Gold;
- Roses Design Awards 2006 – Website – Gold;
- CIPR North West Awards 2006 – Grand Prix.

KEY LESSONS

In reviewing the success of Chimney Pot Park sales launch, a number of lessons can be drawn from the campaign, including:

- In the property sector like any other, public relations can be used creatively to build interest and stimulate demand, in this case through a highly effective combination of direct prospect communication, media relations and event management.
- It also shows the importance of good quality images and photography to support public relations activity. In property, developments are often sold before they are built so having great images that bring architects' designs to life capture the imagination of buyers and the press alike.
- Chimney Pot Park also highlights how an integrated approach to public relations, marketing and sales can lead to strong results. If public relations had been working

in isolation at Urban Splash, the early flourish of press coverage would have dampened interest in the story at the times of the sales launch. By not issuing any proactive press releases until the launch date announcement, Urban Splash was able to control the press coverage (as much as possible).

Index